THE
TRUTH
ABOUT
POSITIVE
CASH FLOW
PROPERTY

THE
TRUTH
ABOUT
POSITIVE
CASH FLOW
PROPERTY

Margaret Lomas

Wrightbooks

First published 2006 by Wrightbooks
an imprint of John Wiley & Sons Australia, Ltd
42 McDougall Street, Milton, Qld 4064

Offices also in Sydney and Melbourne

Typeset in 11/14 pt Berkeley

Reprinted December 2006

© Margaret Lomas 2006

The moral rights of the author have been asserted.

National Library of Australia Cataloguing-in-Publication data:

Lomas, Margaret.

The truth about positive cash flow.

Includes index.

ISBN 0 7314 0456 4.

1. Real estate investment - Australia. 2. Real property -
Australia. 3. Cash management - Australia. I. Title.

332.63240994

Cover design by Rob Cowpe

Printed in Australia by McPherson's Printing Group

10 9 8 7 6 5 4 3 2

Disclaimer

Contents

To Reuben

To find the partner of your soul only happens once in a lifetime, if at all. Not only have I found mine in you, but you have stayed with me through the tough times.
I love you now and forever.

Acknowledgments

I would like to acknowledge the following people who have made my life so much easier and who mean so much to me:

Mum — I know you miss Dad (as I still do), but you have shown such amazing strength since he passed. Happy 80th birthday! I love you.

Karyn — thanks for your support this past year when I needed it most. You can't know what it means to me.

Teresa — I hope I have mentioned you in each book. What would I do without you?

The Destiny® head office team — we are blessed to have such a special group of wonderful people to drive the Destiny® machine. Thank you all so much for your efforts.

All of my branch managers — every one of you provides our clients with such special care and attention and treat them as if they are family. I couldn't ask for more, and thank you all so much for taking on this task with such commitment and enthusiasm.

All of my children:
Mark — who has striven so hard this year — I am proud of you.
Kristy — away overseas for almost a year and now a lovely, loving young woman with a great career ahead of you. Belinda, Belly — the gorgeous butterfly who comes home occasionally to kiss her mother.
Michael — almost a man but still such a wonderful boy deep inside.
And Becky — where did our baby go? A beautiful high school girl with the biggest heart I have ever seen. I love you all so much.

Noel Whittaker and Nell Jenman — you are both my mentors, guiding lights for me which help me to keep my own personal ethics intact.

Finally, Dad — of course, I still miss you. Three years and the memories have not faded even a tiny bit. I think I am who I am today because of you. Thank you.

What people say about Margaret's books:

*I have just finished reading **How to Maximise Your Property Portfolio**, having also read **How to Create an Income for Life**.*

I have to tell you that I have been searching for this type of information for quite a while. It was pure pleasure reading your books, knowing that I had finally found someone who is able to look at property investing from a holistic viewpoint and who has a thorough understanding of the subject. Your ability to communicate this information simply and clearly is commendable and I found I was able to easily follow and understand what you were saying.

My goal has been to have 20 investment properties before retirement and I now know how to achieve this goal, thanks to you. I would just like to say thank you! Thank you so much for putting sanity into the otherwise insane practice of property investing.

Kim Ayers

*I have just finished reading your book **How to Create an Income for Life** for the second time, and I cannot commend you highly enough for putting together such an easy-to-read and even easier to understand guide to positive cash flow property!*

Thank you for taking the time to share your wealth of knowledge on the investing topic with the general public, without people like you who want to help others learn and succeed, it would be so difficult for people like myself to even know where to start! After reading your book, I feel that much of the fear and uncertainty created by a lack of knowledge has been buried forever, and I am even more excited about property investment as an option for securing our future than I ever thought possible.

Sally Hudson

It all started with your book back in 2001 … I have to pinch myself from time to time! I thought it was time that I thanked you for your books, particularly the first one, which got me started.

My wife Rosalie thanks you also. She was very apprehensive about retirement, just couldn't see how we would get by!

She is once again the woman I married, we are both freed from the financial burdens that plague the general populace. When I whistle while I work, people look at me strangely. Is being contented a lost sense?

Thank you and keep up the good work. I promote your books to everyone I come in contact with.

Chris and Rosalie Vine

Thank you so very much for sharing your wisdom, knowledge and experience with everyone. Through your efforts and the domino effect, you are going to be responsible for improving the future lives of many, many people, all over the world, mine included.

Thanks so much Margaret for your work and support in the world of investing.

Gary and Kathy Klarendeck

*What a happy task it is to say that I was delighted to read your book **A Pocket Guide to Positive Cash Flow**. I found it informative and easy to read and understand. Well done!*

PR

Thanks again for being such an inspiration.

SC

I have found your book easy to understand and look forward to reading your others … thank you for sharing your knowledge with people like myself. I don't know if you could ever realise how much hope you have given me.

I hope I am right in saying that you have written your books because you really care. One day may I be able to give some of this back to somebody else.

SS

Out of all the people I've come into contact with in the property industry, you are the only one I would really trust. Good on you, Margaret!

PM

*Just finished reading **How to Create an Income for Life** — a great book, Margaret! It really brings property investing into perspective and I learnt a lot from it. Unlike other books that leave you feeling as though you can make a million in a few months, this book sticks to reality and, sometimes, reality sucks! But it is real and having read several books on the subject, this is one of the best I've read to date. Well done, Margaret!*

DF

*I have just finished reading your book **How to Create an Income for Life** and loved it. I have read quite a few investment books and found yours to be the most inspiring. I really came out of every chapter feeling uplifted (unlike a lot of the others I have read).*

SG

Introduction

A short time ago, we were driving in the car with our 11-year-old daughter Rebecca, who sat in the back seat happily sketching her surroundings. As my husband Reuben and I are often inclined to do, we were discussing our property portfolio, our plans for additional purchases, the general state of our borrowings and myriad other things. At some point in the journey, one of us made a comment about the debt we had attached to the properties we owned.

On hearing this, Rebecca suddenly became aware of us and asked in a worried voice, 'Why do you owe so much money to the bank? Don't you own the properties yourself?'

I thought about how I could explain this to her in a way she would understand.

'Well,' I began, 'Mummy and Daddy don't have enough money to buy as many properties that we have by ourselves, so we asked the bank to help us out.'

'But what good is that?' she countered. 'You have to give the money back to the bank sometime!'

How do you explain this to a young person without going into lengthy detail about tax breaks, tenants covering interest repayments, growth, cash flow, leverage and all of the other important characteristics of property investing today?

'Okay,' I said to her. 'It works like this. Let's say we buy a property for $100 000. The bank gives us $100 000. After five years, the property is worth more because things always cost more in the future. Let's imagine we sell it then and we get $130 000 for it. We give the $100 000 back to the bank, and we keep the $30 000 for ourselves.

Now let's think about buying lots of properties. Say we bought 20 instead of just one, and we had the same result. After five years, we sell them all and pay the bank back the $2 million we owe it. We get to keep the $600 000 left over.'

Just as the sun rises on a crisp summer morning, Rebecca's face lit up with understanding as she processed this information. With all of the innocence only youth can have, she exclaimed, 'Why doesn't everyone do that, then?'

At that, Reuben and I both burst out laughing and replied, 'We don't know!'

And we don't! Sure, it's not quite as simple as I made out to Rebecca, and the process of buying property as an investment is a complex, time consuming and, occasionally, risky venture. But, if you learn how to invest well in property, work out how to sort the wheat from the chaff in terms of strategy and commit yourself to a solid plan, the bottom line really is as simple as Rebecca believed it to be—with a careful and considered approach, you really can make money using other people's funds.

I have always loved property and have written four books about it. I admit that when I wrote the first book, I was somewhat naïve. I was full of hope that what I had discovered in the early years and which seemed to be working would stand the test of time, delivering the means by which Reuben and I could one day retire from the paid workforce and fulfil many of the dreams we share. Looking back, I was quite an upstart and it was rather arrogant to actually think that my small amount of success should be shared with the country at large. Yet, much of what I wrote was really just common sense.

Today our portfolio comprises 30 properties and we are looking for the next few as I write. I now possess the benefit of time and the wisdom of experience and I can honestly tell you that positive cash flow property investment does work. I can also tell you that there is no magic formula, it is not quick and there are no secrets involved. Over time, there have been many things I thought might work which haven't, but the basics of successful property investing remain unchanged, despite what the 'property investment industry' might tell us today.

You only need three things to get yourself ready to start out in property investing—time, perseverance and courage. I can't give you those three things—you need to possess them already. If you do have them, then this book, along with the books in my *How to* series and support from truly independent and qualified investment property advisers are all the tools you will need to make your goals a reality. Arm yourself with decent, proven education, and then forge headlong into the future. You have very little to lose, and much to gain!

Margaret Lomas

February 2006

Chapter 1

The truth about positive cash flow property

Great expectations

If you are reading this book, it is probably because you want to know how to get ahead using property as your vehicle. You may be hoping to make a quick gain from buying and selling property, or you may have the long-term goal of creating a portfolio of properties from which you can generate a retirement income.

Whatever your personal goal is, it is highly likely that you have already been bombarded with a plethora of information from many sources and at present you are a little unsure about where to head.

A few weeks ago, I had a conversation with a client who had been investing in property for almost two years. When we had first met, Maurie and his wife owned a lovely home in Sydney on which they still had quite a large mortgage. They had around 40 per cent equity and, due to the fact that they had three quite young children, they did not really have any money available to invest. They had decided that property was a good option for them and were looking for a way to obtain a portfolio of property that would allow them to retire in 10 years' time at age 55, without straining their already over-stretched budget today.

Maurie had done a great job over the two years and was in the process of acquiring his fifth property. He had read all of the books I have written and followed the strategies I profess. He had decided, however, to augment his knowledge by attending a weekend workshop (cleverly called a 'masterclass', no doubt to lift its status) being held by a self-professed 'guru' of positive cash flow property.

After the weekend, Maurie called me in great alarm to ask what I thought about the rather dubious strategy he had been taught that weekend (and upon which I will expand later in this book). Since I was of the opinion that Maurie was already doing a superb job in achieving his goals, I asked why he was considering this new approach and what had motivated his call to me.

'The course presenter has bought literally hundreds of properties using this great new technique, and at the rate I am progressing I am simply never going to get ahead quickly enough. I have to get moving!' he told me.

Before I tackle the nuts and bolts of this book, let me say I am thoroughly sick and tired of these self-styled 'experts' who are causing unnecessary anxiety among hardworking Australians and promoting, usually for their own financial gain, a multitude of risky, often illegal and usually impossible to achieve 'get rich quick' schemes. Most of these strategies achieve nothing other than landing honest people in trouble, and sooner or later many such promoters are investigated by ASIC and sometimes criminally charged for their activities. It makes my blood positively boil when I see another 'authority', along with the Ferrari and the adoring disciples, splashed across the media, espousing all manner of magical strategies to the growing population of 'almost retired' who are desperate to make some kind of difference to their future prosperity.

Like never before, it seems that the innocent are being preyed upon by the cleverly dishonest. The increasing concern over our financial futures, which is fuelled by a government unable to promise lasting welfare benefits for the aged, has become the basis upon which these immoral opportunists unleash their next wealth creation scheme.

Before reading on, be aware of some very important things:

1. People have been making good profits from property in this country for more than 100 years and none of them ever needed to uncover any 'secret' or use any magic formula.

2. Since I first wrote about positive cash flow property in 2001, I have yet to come across any 'expert' who truly understands what positive cash flow property is all about or how you can best go about finding it and making money from it. The 'experts' rarely understand the concept and generally use it very loosely and, usually, incorrectly.

3. Few of these experts are able to demonstrate that they have successfully used for themselves the strategies they are teaching you. Almost all of them have made their money selling these concepts to you at outrageous prices and preying on the less-educated.

4. You do not need to have a huge portfolio of properties to retire with an excellent income stream. The average person can, with a little time on his or her side, build a retirement income equal to at least five times the old age pension, with only 10 properties. There is simply no need to have higher expectations than that, although once you do have 10 properties in your portfolio, you will find it

fairly easy to build on that and you will most likely want to continue to buy and build.

5. Slow and steady wins the race. This has always been the case and, as proverbs go, it is still a good one and applies to property investing today. You must not be frightened into taking action that is ultimately risky for you and that will not, in all probability, pay off. There are very few real experts in this country today who can show you how to safely and successfully build a retirement income through property investing. It is more than likely that anyone spruiking his or her wares via expensive seminars or costly software programs is peddling strategies that simply cannot work for you over the long term. In the main, these strategies and seminars do make money—for the presenters, who probably have no assets of their own and are poised to flee as soon as their unscrupulous activities are uncovered.

Education is the key

Now that I have that off my chest, let's get into some good, solid, old-fashioned education. This book is designed to answer all of those little questions you may have about investing in property. I have written it to help expose the untruths you may have heard elsewhere, and to show that you can in fact build a successful portfolio of properties without taking large risks or undertaking strategies that may be illegal today, or are the result of a tax loophole that is sure to be closed at some time in the future.

Before you read this book

It is crucial that, in order to grasp the basics of how to successfully invest in true positive cash flow property, you read one of the books in my *How to* series, plus *A Pocket Guide to Investing in Positive Cash Flow Property*. These books will provide you with the important information you need to understand—and then acquire—property as an investment. Since each of my books is different and is designed for investors at different stages of their investing life, at the end of this book I have outlined their contents and who they are meant for.

Once you have educated yourself about positive cash flow property and you are fully conversant in the process you must follow to buy it, you will then be ready to read this book. It will fill in any blanks and go a long way toward protecting you from the clutches of the unscrupulous people you will no doubt meet along the way. It will answer questions as they arise and ensure that you know everything there is to know about positive cash flow property—its pitfalls, its benefits and its ability to build a viable future income for you. This is all information you can really only absorb and truly understand once the process has begun for you—hence the need to start with one of the other books.

Let's begin by covering some important ground that all of the other books have also covered. It is the starting point from which we will launch into the murky waters of the problems and concerns you will most likely encounter during your journey. If you are confident that you fully understand positive cash flow property, you might like to skip ahead to the next chapter. Otherwise, a review at this point may not be a bad idea.

What is positive cash flow property?

This week I read an article in a newsletter prepared by the founder of a fairly well-known 'club' for property investors. Despite his own very shady past (information freely available in the public domain), this fellow took it upon himself to lambast an interview I had done for the Qantas *Business on Q* radio program.

I am happy to bear scrutiny at any time and answer questions people may have about the concepts I teach; however, it is a different story when someone chooses to denigrate you on grounds that are simply not accurate. Sadly for this gentleman, not only were all of the points he took me to task on incorrect (he based his criticisms on misquotes and misinterpretations, as well as just plain untruths), he also clearly demonstrated his own lack of understanding of positive cash flow property.

The latter flaw is not uncommon, however, and today people are using the term 'positive cash flow' to describe all manners of property investing, even those that are simply not 'positive cash flow' investing at all. To completely understand positive cash flow property investing, let us first take a look at what is it not.

Negative gearing

Until recently, 'negative gearing' was the most commonly recognised term in the property investment industry. Everyone knows someone who has bought 'negatively geared' property in the past, yet few people understand what the term truly means.

To understand that there are better ways to invest in property, it is essential that you comprehend negative gearing, the principles of which form the basis for knowing how to generate a positive cash flow from property. *How to Create an Income for Life* (chapter 2, page 14) has a detailed description of gearing for property investors that will take you through each step of this very important concept.

In a nutshell, negative gearing means 'borrowing for a loss'. 'Gearing' is the term used to describe the process of borrowing funds to buy a greater amount of growth assets, or to gain a greater exposure to a growth market. When you negatively gear, your borrowings, and the yearly expenses of the investment, exceed the income you make. The tax office takes pity on you (a very rare occurrence!) and allows you to claim this loss against income you have earned from other sources. The loss effectively reduces your total income for the year, which means that you can have back some of the tax you've paid as your actual 'taxable' income is less than it was before you bought the property. This 'tax break' pays for some of the loss (up to 45 per cent, depending on your personal marginal rate of tax), but you must pay the difference (55 per cent) from your personal funds.

Let's look at an example. In the main, a property will return to you around 4 per cent to 5 per cent of its purchase price as a yearly income. So, if you buy a property that costs you $150 000, you can expect to receive around $7500 a year in rent. In some areas of Australia, you can receive higher returns than this, while some will bring considerably lower ones. In addition, if you buy property in the larger cities, you will probably pay a lot more for the property and receive a considerably lower relative rent return. In essence, wherever you buy, the more you pay for a property, the lower the relative rent return you can expect to receive. This is because the large variance in property prices is not countered with an equally large variance in rent returns—rents tend not to vary at such a great rate within an area.

If you assumed that interest rates are 7 per cent and that you borrowed the entire purchase price, and that yearly investment costs on the property (such as rates, insurance and management fees) are another 2 per cent, then a property such as the one above would generally cost you around $13 500 to maintain. You would then be in the position of having to make up the difference ($6000) from your personal funds and your tax breaks. The maximum tax break on a $6000 loss would be

$2700, so you would be required to pay the balance of $3300 (approximately $60 a week) from your own pocket.

Why do people do this? Many people choose to do it as a way of reducing their tax bill. They would rather pay an extra $60 a week on a property that may (or may not) increase in value over time than they would pay the money to the tax department. High-income earners often use this strategy to reduce what is considered to be a high tax bill.

Hoping for high growth

Other people choose investments with the above characteristics out of a belief that low-income property usually shows a higher growth because its low returns means it is extremely well-located (and so the purchase price was very high). You will find the highest value properties in capital cities around Australia, but in almost every case they have the lowest comparative rent return. This means that, in order to buy property that may grow faster (assuming that capital cities grow faster than other areas), you must accept a lower rent return and therefore a higher commitment to the difference between the actual loss and the tax break you receive. The desired outcome for those working to this plan is that the property will increase in value greatly enough to recompense them for this loss over time.

The reality, however, is that once you consider buying and selling costs and capital gains tax, as well as the loss in value of money over time and the lost opportunity (that is, you didn't have the cash you were putting in to the property to invest elsewhere), often the increased value doesn't really cover the high output. In addition, people buying property hoping for high growth must sell the property in the future to get their money back. Sometimes, if the timing is not right, they may be forced to sell at the wrong time, such as during a lull, and so the expected return may never materialise.

I won't argue with the school of thought that says that good growth property is found within 10 kilometres of the CBD, as some property experts will espouse. It is certainly true that, for as long as we can remember, property within 10 kilometres and often 20 kilometres of large cities grows very well over time and, for those lucky few who can afford it, can provide a tidy sum for retirement.

What I will assert, however, is that few people can afford to obtain, and then maintain, a substantial portfolio of these low return, potentially high growth properties. Yes, some people may be able to commit $60 a week, some even more than that, in order to buy blue-chip properties that have every chance of good growth. But the question must be asked—how many of these properties can one buy, if any? I spend my days talking to people who barely have enough cash to survive today, what with the rising costs of fuel and decent education for their children. Many of them, like me, have negative cash flow children! We are all still waiting for the return on that investment, but while we have them we certainly do not have enough spare cash to be injecting into a property portfolio. These are people whose budgets simply cannot afford the strain of an extra $60 or $120 a week, all in the hope that in the future the properties will rise enough in value to provide the retirement nest egg they require.

So what should they do? Is it better to do nothing because they cannot afford potentially high growth property, or is it better to find another way, one that is probably just as profitable (perhaps even more so) once you know what you are doing?

I will show you, at various stages in this book, how anyone, regardless of whether their budgets are in surplus or deficit, can buy property without the financial burden today, and put together a solid growth portfolio with a very low risk. I will also show you how, while it may be true that capital cities do indeed deliver high growth to investors, this does not mean that the reverse is true. Areas other than capital cities can also deliver high growth, with the added benefit of higher proportionate returns and cash flow today. This powerful combination can add up to be a very profitable strategy for those who learn how to use it well.

Positive gearing

High rent returns

In the olden days (which, according to my children, was when I was born), it was possible to find many areas in Australia where the rent return you received on a property was considerably more for each dollar you invested than the national average. While property in traditional growth areas (such as capital cities and large regional areas) provided up to 5 per cent (of the purchase price) per annum as a rent return, there were areas in this country where the return was well above this, sometimes as high as 9 and 10 per cent and often much higher than this.

Typically, properties such as these were located in towns and regional areas that were based on one industry, such as mining or timber milling. Because of that, the population was largely itinerant, and there was a huge demand from tenants and a small demand from buyers. The result of this was that rent returns would skyrocket while property values remained stagnant, and so the disparity between rent return and purchase price grew more and more.

During this time, certain clever people jumped in and bought up large parcels of property in these towns. They were able to buy blocks of units for impossibly low prices and command ridiculous rent returns. It was not uncommon for an investor to purchase a block of six units for $25 000, and then receive $80 a week rent return for each unit (a total of $480, or 99 per cent return). These people continued this success in many similar areas and so put together very large portfolios of properties in a very short time. They made wonderful returns and while they paid tax on these returns (as the gains they made were all net 'taxable' gains), the balance after tax was still substantial, often allowing them to repay debt at an alarming speed and so leverage again and again.

Sadly, for investors, this situation was never going to be sustainable and today properties such as these are as rare as hen's teeth. The clever investors went on to write books about purchasing huge numbers of properties in short periods of time, and so the jig was up and the word was out. Investors flocked to such areas in search of similar bargains and, as the age-old economic principle of supply and demand will dictate, demand soon began to outstrip supply and prices inevitably rose as quickly as the rent returns did. The problem of insufficient buyers ceased to exist as out-of-town investors saw the potential and pushed prices up, despite the lack of demand from local purchasers.

Today it is an impossible dream to find such huge rent returns for such low prices, and while there are still areas which do indeed return a higher than average rental income for the price paid, the huge returns of old are simply not achievable anymore. In those few areas where you can still snap up cheaper properties with big returns, the risk is much higher—the concentration of labour in one, often unstable, industry means that a future for these towns cannot be guaranteed.

So let's be very clear—positive cash flow property is not about positive gearing, although it is one form of positive cash flow investing and it does have its place in some portfolios. It is not about finding the high returns for the low prices. It is far more complex than that, and this is probably why so few 'experts' understand themselves what true cash flow investing is all about.

Large deposit

I remember reading an article last year that brought a smile to my face. It was written by a real estate agent who had taken it upon himself to become a 'property investment adviser'. The article waxed lyrical about positive gearing and how it was the only way someone should invest in property. It then went on to uncover the secret of positive gearing as if it were the greatest revelation ever, about to be disclosed for the first time.

'Quite simply,' it said, more or less, 'the larger the deposit you can bring into the purchase, the higher your cash flow will be. So, if you want to buy a $200 000 property, and you can bring in $100 000 of your own money, you will reduce your expenses (as in 'loan interest costs') and increase your cash flow.'

While it is wonderful to see real estate agents genuinely attempting to educate their clients, they are usually not financial advisers and do not have the qualifications to enable them to adequately assist investors in this way. Any advice they give to you will be limited. In relation to this particular piece of advice, any and every property would have a positive cash flow for every investor if they could simply raise enough cash to minimise their borrowings.

But there's the crunch—who can raise that kind of cash? And, if you could, would property be the best place to put it all? I am a financial adviser and I believe in spreading my money over several asset classes. I am happy to continually borrow the money from the bank to build my property portfolio, as I consider this to be a prudent way to leverage the equity that continues to accrue into more growth assets. But when it comes to the money my husband and I earn from the work we do, I like to spread that around a little, and keep it relatively available if we need it in a hurry. In fact, I personally do not like to use any of our available cash for property, choosing instead to use that in other, more liquid investments, while I use our constantly increasing property equity to buy more property. Later in this book, I will discuss more about equity, debt reduction and leverage, but for now, understand that positive cash flow is not about having a big deposit. Building a substantial property portfolio is about knowing how to leverage from one property to the next by purchasing property which not only looks after itself in terms of its expenses, but which also provides extra cash for you to invest back into the portfolio, gaining equity more quickly so you can buy more property sooner.

Will the real positive cash flow property please stand up?

We have established that positive cash flow property is not about big rent returns. It's not about big deposits. Then what else is there?

I receive email and calls from people every week telling me that they simply cannot find positive cash flow property, or that it no longer exists. When I ask them how they are searching, they usually tell me that they have logged on to the internet and used one of the property search websites such as www.realestate.com.au. Usually, on further questioning, these people will reveal that, in order to work out the cash flows, they have taken the purchase price, added a sum for purchase costs, added 2 per cent or so for yearly costs and then worked out if the rent return will cover the entire outgo.

Wrong! A true positive cash flow property is not necessarily recognisable when you first look for it, simply because many people do not fully understand the impact of on-paper costs. Let's take this one step at a time, and start from the beginning.

Getting that cash flow

In 1985, the tax office changed some of its rules where property investors were concerned. Basically, these changes meant that if an investor purchased a property constructed after 18 July 1985, he or she was allowed to claim depreciation for the building itself, as well as all of the fixtures, fittings and furniture contained within. To put this more simply, the tax office allowed investors to claim the loss of value on the property (not the land, which of course gains value), and be compensated for this loss by redeeming some of the tax they had paid on other income.

Imagine you purchased a property, originally built in 1998, for which you paid $160 000. Of that $160 000, a quantity surveyor assesses that the actual original building value is $80 000, and a further $40 000 represents the current value of the fixtures, fittings and furniture (more detail on allowable deductions in chapter 9). The remaining $40 000 is the present value of the land.

For tax purposes, you may claim 2.5 per cent of the loss of the original value (depreciation) of the building every year for 40 years. The fixtures, fittings and furniture have varying rates of depreciation depending on the item and its current value, but let's make an assumption that the average life of an item is around seven years (some are more and some are less). For tax purposes, the total loss in value of this property would be $2000 for the building and $5714 per annum (for seven years) for the rest. In total, you claim a loss in value of $7714. (Be aware that at this point you do not have to pay out anything for this—it is a loss in 'value' only. Of course, in the future when some of these items on which you are claiming a loss really do wear out, you will have to replace them, but we will deal with how this is managed later in chapter 9. For now, let's just consider that you now have an amount of $7714 for which you can claim a tax deduction.)

Just say you receive a rent return of $230 per week for this property. You pay out $3000 a year in property costs and $11 150 a year in interest (at 7 per cent). At this point, your income and expenses look like table 1.1.

Table 1.1: income and expenses

	Income	Expenses
	$11 960 *(rent)*	$11 150 *(interest)*
		$3000 *(costs)*
Total:	**$11 960**	**$14 150**

At first glance, it looks like you have lost $2190. Before we complete this equation, however, we have to consider the tax breaks.

If we assume a tax bracket of 30 per cent (as this captures most people these days), this $2190 loss will result in a tax refund of $657. But let's not forget about the loss of value, or depreciation, outlined previously. This came to a total of $7714, and at the 30 per cent marginal rate of tax, this will bring in an extra tax refund of $2314. So how do we look now in terms of what comes in and what goes out? See table 1.2.

Table 1.2: income and expenses, with tax

	Income	Expenses
	$11 960 *(rent)*	$11 150 *(interest)*
$\left(14,150 - 11,960\right)(.3) =$ $657 *(tax refund on actual loss)*		$3000 *(costs)*
	$2314 *(tax refund on depreciation)*	
Total:	**$14 931**	**$14 150**

15

Not only has this property covered its own costs, it has also provided an extra $781 per annum ($15 per week) over and above this.

It's easy to see why people say that you cannot find positive cash flow property anymore. What they really mean is that you cannot find positively geared property anymore. Determining whether a property is likely to have a positive cash flow requires you to carry out a range of calculations that are based on the ultimate purchase price and rent return, as well as the possible on-paper deductions it may bring for you. I have tried to make this process a little more simple by providing each reader with free software, available from the Destiny® Financial Solutions website at www.destiny.net.au. While it uses 'rule of thumb' calculations to establish on-paper deductions, it can give you some idea of the possible deductions you may be eligible for, so that you can come closer to determining if a property has the potential to deliver the cash flow you need to make it work for you.

The added benefits

While many people say they can afford to commit hard-earned dollars to their property portfolio, and so have no trouble buying negatively geared property, positive cash flow property brings with it some added benefits, over and above the cash flow.

Interest rate rises

When interest rates rise, people who have to commit $20 or $40 a week to their property portfolios suffer. I have seen cases where an unexpected interest rate rise has forced people to sell prematurely, often years before their strategy has paid off with growth. These people may have ascertained that they can afford the weekly commitment, but when rate rises add an extra $20 or $30 a week, the story changes.

When you buy property with a positive cash flow, you build in a margin that can help you manage interest rate rises. While a rate rise will eat into your cash flow from the property, at least you have a cash flow to eat into! Your personal budgets may not need to suffer at all.

Vacancy rates

The same can be said for those periods of vacancy. A negatively geared property that has $250-a-week rent and a $40-a-week commitment on the owner's part, cannot afford to suffer any periods without a tenant. For each week without a tenant, $5 (less the 30 per cent tax break for this increased loss) is added to the yearly loss.

A positive cash flow property with the same rent return but a $20-a-week net cash flow can withstand at least four weeks' (six weeks once the extra tax break is received) vacancy every year. Positive cash flow property does provide a pretty good hedge against the risk of vacancy.

Debt reduction

When you have property that gives you a positive cash flow, you have extra money each week to do with as you wish. Smart investors will cycle this cash flow straight back into their debt, as not only will this pay the debt off sooner, it will also provide interest offset, thereby reducing the interest paid on the debt.

To build a large portfolio, you must be able to leverage off the growing equity of your property. People who negatively gear probably only have the equity created by market growth, as the weekly loss usually makes it impossible for these investors to do anything more than make interest repayments on the debt.

Those who choose positive cash flow property have extra money to service their debts. In addition to gaining equity from value increases, they gain equity through debt repayment. Please remember the following piece of important information:

For every $1 of property you own, that's
$5 worth of property you can buy through leverage.

This means that, since the bank will lend you $4 for every $1 you have in savings or in property equity, repaying debt as a means to speeding up property acquisition is a crucial part of the plan. Later in this book, you will read some real-life illustrations of how investors in positive cash flow property, who undertake a strategy for rapid mortgage reduction, can speed up their property acquisition.

Summary

- You do not need to buy hundreds or even dozens of properties to put together a sound retirement income.

- There are no secret formulas or tax loopholes to make you 'rich' from property. Hard work and research can, however, ensure you set up a healthy retirement income.

- When you buy property that requires a weekly commitment from your own pocket, there is a limit to the number of properties you can buy. Even if they skyrocket in value, you cannot leverage against this increase if you have no more disposable income to commit to your strategy.

- When you buy positive cash flow property, you can afford to hold it through the tough times because you have a margin built in. Even if you experience lower growth because you have bought property in smaller, low growth areas, your cash flow will help you gain equity in the property through debt repayment, so you can leverage against this equity.

- Be careful of anyone who claims to be any kind of property investment expert. If there is a major financial gain from their 'advice' (such as the ridiculous fees charged for 'seminars' or commissions if you buy their properties) or if they have no real qualifications, then it is likely that their clever strategies are designed to make money for them, not you.

Conclusion

There is much more to know about positive cash flow property and this information is covered in later chapters. For now, be sure that you are careful who you listen to and question what they say to gauge whether they really do understand the true meaning of positive cash flow. Most importantly, understand that the ability of any property to have a positive cash flow is property-based more than it is area-based—it depends on the on-paper deductions of the individual property. This means that any location may have a mix of both negatively geared and positive cash flow properties because it will be the characteristics of any one property that makes it predisposed to positive cash flow. Knowing this means that you do not have to find areas where rent returns are high—you have to find properties with a high amount of depreciation and solid rent returns.

To become a leader in property investing, you have to be a pioneer. An investor with herd mentality will follow the crowd and invest where everyone else is investing. He or she will ask supposed 'experts' where to invest, and will spend time trying to learn the latest technique or tax loophole to bring them riches.

A pioneer will learn how to recognise positive cash flow property for him- or herself. He or she will acquire the important skills needed to seek out and acquire viable property long before anyone else knows it exists, and so be the one to snap up the bargains before the 'boom'. Pioneers will know that education, care and time will eventually lead to success and that a few well-bought and sound properties, purchased on the basis of viable information will far outperform many hastily bought properties relying on the latest scheme or idea.

Chapter 2

Location, location
— or not?

_____

Property and the 'yuck' factor

I actually wanted this to be the title of this book, but an overwhelming majority of people vetoed the idea! They all thought it would send the wrong message and I guess, since I have been misquoted a number of times now, they may be right.

In the last chapter, I discussed how crucial it is to ensure that when you buy property, you are able to generate a positive cash flow. This is because it is only through cash flow that you are able to leverage. Cash flow not only allows you to hold on to the property today, as you do not need to make a personal commitment to retaining it, it also allows you to have extra cash to inject into your borrowings and this creates equity more quickly. Equity equals leverage in the first instance and, later, represents increased income.

Many people believe that my strategy is to buy property in small country towns or in areas where no-one wants to live, so that I can acquire cheap real estate. This cannot be any further from the truth and the process I apply to buying is complex and requires a huge amount of research. It has turned out, however, that this process has uncovered some properties which, *at present*, may be in areas where the locals would not necessarily choose to live. This is only because my research has uncovered very important characteristics that led me to believe that change may be on the horizon.

I recall being at an expo in Perth on a weekend we settled on a property we had bought there. The area was around 25 minutes' drive from the CBD and consisted of first homebuyers on lower incomes, and renters. Our research indicated that extensions of the freeway, planned infrastructure and spiralling property prices in Perth would mean that in the future, the area had the potential to become a growth suburb. Already it was showing a marked growth in population, and land for new building was becoming scarce.

I had been on the radio the morning before the expo and mentioned that we had purchased property in Perth. Inevitably, most visitors to the expo eagerly wanted to know exactly where we had bought. On almost every occasion, when I mentioned the suburb people looked at me aghast, and exclaimed, 'Why on earth would you buy *there*?'

These days, as I travel around the country, I ask people in capital cities to remember the suburbs that years ago no-one liked. I personally was never allowed to go through Redfern on a train for fear of my abduction, and now that they have changed parts of that suburb to 'Strawberry Hills', it has become the place to be. Brisbane has seen dramatically rising prices in the previously unpopular suburbs of Redcliffe and Deception Bay, while Adelaide locals tell me that, years ago, Henley Beach was definitely not the sought after area it is today. Look around your own town or city and you will see many, many suburbs that, although previously undesirable, have skyrocketed in value, often for no apparent reason.

The Perth property we purchased two years ago has increased in value from the $120 000 we paid to $290 000, which is a 141 per cent increase in two years. In addition, we were able to chop off the unnecessarily large backyard and build a second dwelling for just $120 000, and it too is now worth $290 000. Total purchase price—$240 000; total value today—$580 000! Not bad for a 'yuck' suburb!

Of course, this does not always happen. But if you follow a few simple rules, you have every chance of being able to buy property that others may reject today, which tomorrow rises in value at a greater speed than the average. There are a few important points to remember:

1. As prices in a city or town increase, people are forced to begin moving out of town or to suburbs other than those where they were raised.

2. Over a period of 10 to 15 years, the demographics of entire areas can, and will, change dramatically. For example, areas previously consisting of state (welfare) housing will begin to attract first homebuyers as they are sold off and are no longer available only to welfare recipients. Often when an area or suburb has too many undesirable characteristics, the local council will spend money in an effort to change this. There are countless suburbs in many states where councils have spent millions of dollars on beautification projects that subsequently attract a different demographic.

3. People will commute to work for as long as an hour and, in large capital cities, 1.5 hours. It is prudent to consider

areas that today seem as though they are isolated but that have, or will have (due to planned infrastructure), reliable transport to the nearest large town or city. When a boom hits an area or town, a subsequent boom often ensues years later in surrounding areas.

4. Councils can provide much information about population growth and planned infrastructure. Always find out what is planned for the future when considering an area in which to buy.

When you take these factors into consideration, you become a little more visionary. As I have already mentioned, people who follow others will only ever have marginal success. But those who can put aside their biases will be the people who may just discover the next major boom area. They will be the people talked about in years to come as having been lucky enough to 'be in the right place at the right time'.

Important characteristics

In chapter 3 of *A Pocket Guide to Investing in Positive Cash Flow Property*, I outlined 20 must-ask questions that are crucial to every real estate transaction. The answers to these questions make up the bulk of the research that must be carried out to maximise your success as a property investor. If you have not read these 20 questions, be sure to do so now as they contain vital information. So often, I receive email from readers saying, 'I found a property with a $50-a-week positive cash flow. Do you think I should buy it?' Since the amount of cash flow is only question 1, my answer is always, 'I don't know, what did you discover when you considered the other 19 questions?'

No property should be even contemplated unless every one of these questions has been asked and satisfactorily answered, and knowing these questions means you never have to rely on the opinion of others to make a purchase decision. The right property will present itself to you when it satisfies all of the necessary criteria covered in the 20 questions.

However, before even delving that deeply, there are a few basic characteristics that an area must have before you should spend any time searching for property there. Areas with potential have a reasonable population, economic vibrancy and little vacant land still available. These attributes are discussed below.

Reasonable population

I like an area to have a growing population, with at least 15 000 people already living there permanently. I might consider an area with a little less than this amount if it can show sustained population growth over the past 10 years. I will also consider areas with a population as little as 5000, but only if it is less than 30 minutes' commute to a major city, regional area or town. This is because, as previously mentioned, people will commute and people who work in town often choose to live outside it.

Economic vibrancy

I need to be reassured that the town in question is thriving, whatever its size. A flourishing town has new businesses, low vacancy on commercial premises and is 'self-sufficient'—in other words, it has all of the major services (such as supermarkets and cinemas) in town. Any town without these characteristics has limited chance for growth in the future, as there is little to lure more residents.

Little vacant land available

Where there is ample vacant land, your property will not increase in value as quickly, as people often prefer building something new over buying an existing property. Little available land results in upward pressure on the prices of existing properties (as long as there is a growing population and all other factors are present).

Don't forget, there are 20 questions to be asked and the above criteria should only be used to prioritise the areas where you will concentrate your effort. Once you have narrowed down somewhere that looks to be shaping up as an area that is viable for continued investing success, you will be ready to delve more deeply and carry out the bulk of the important research.

But I don't *know* the area

When most people are looking to buy property as an investment, they tend to cast the net five or 10 kilometres around where they live, and choose to invest there. Having pondered this for many years now, I think the reasons for this are:

1.   They have chosen to live there so it *must* be a good area.

2.   It is far less scary to buy property close to where they live.

3.   They can go and look at it before buying to make sure it's okay.

4.   They can keep an eye on it to ensure the tenants are looking after it, and even drive past every day to check up on it.

Before deciding that you want to invest in property, you must ensure that you have the right mental attitude. This is not a property you are going to live in yourself and your instincts may not be appropriate under these circumstances. In addition, this is not a hobby for you, this is your financial future, and so it is time to put your business hat on and behave in a businesslike manner. If you were about to buy shares in Coles Myer, would you go and visit the different stores, check out the décor and the staff and make your decisions based on what you see? Probably not and the same logic should apply to your property investing—your research and some basic facts will do far more for you than your eyes ever could. That being the case, you must be able to expand your horizons in terms of your search criteria and be aware of the following:

- Your area represents probably less than 1 per cent of the total available opportunities in Australia today. If you insist on buying in your own suburb, town or city, you are missing out on the other 99 per cent of the opportunities.

- When you have one or two properties, it is relatively easy to drive past to check up on them, but what if you build a bigger portfolio? We have 30 properties. If I wanted to drive past them all on my way home from work, I would never get home!

- You must choose to be a property *investor*, not a property manager. For the few after-tax dollars a week it costs to have professional management, it is simply not worth your time to oversee and manage your properties. I admit that property managers can sometimes, for whatever reason, be a problem. However, *A Pocket Guide to Investing in Positive Cash Flow Property* (chapter 7) covers how to recruit and oversee your manager.

- If you insist on looking at all the properties you are potentially going to buy, you are either going to spend a lot of money travelling while you search, or you will buy a lot of property in the one area. Now, although property behaves in cycles, it does not behave in the same cycle all over the country, and when one area booms another plateaus (see later section, next chapter). So, for a good spread and higher than average growth across your entire portfolio, it makes no financial sense to purchase all of your property in the one area.

- If you are worried about not seeing the property before you buy, then don't be. People always ask me how I can buy a property I haven't seen and what if it has some giant problem I will somehow be able to detect by viewing the property before making the purchase. I assure them that even if I looked at it, I probably wouldn't be able to tell that there was a problem—I am not a building inspector and I have no special expertise in this area.

- In reality, all viewing a property can do is make you feel 'good' about it. Feeling 'good' is not a suitable prerequisite for ensuring that the property is viable as an investment! My husband and I have not seen most of the properties we have bought, but I have asked the 20 questions about all of them. Once the 20 questions have been asked, and the relevant pest and building inspections have been done, then there is nothing that looking at the property can do to change its viability as an investment. And when I think of some of the properties we do own, which are growing well and giving us rent every week, I am sure that looking at them would have turned us right off and we never would have purchased them.

Knowing the area

A few years ago, a woman at a function I was speaking at asked me, 'How can you buy property in an area that you don't know? I know my area and so I would rather buy there!'

I asked her a few questions about her area. 'What is the population and its growth?' I asked. 'How much unreleased land is there? What are your council's future plans for development? What is the vacancy rate? Tell me about commercial occupancy.'

Of course, she did not know the answers to these questions. I reassured her that I never buy property in an area I 'don't know'.

While I may never have heard of the area when I first start looking there, by the time I am ready to purchase I am willing to bet that I know the area better than most of the locals.

Positive cash flow property is running out

When speaking to people about investing in positive cash flow property, I am often told that it is running out and that, soon, there will be no more positive cash flow property left in Australia.

This comment presumes that the value of property everywhere is increasing rapidly and consistently, while the rent return on property is increasing slowly (though consistently). If this were the case, then by now, after the country has been established for over 200 years, the price of property everywhere would be astronomical while the rent returns would be so low as to make property investing simply non-viable.

In reality, different areas within the country will come into, and out of, having positive cash flow potential in line with the property cycle of that area.

Generally, the property market will increase in value in a stair-like pattern. Typically, property increases for a time and then plateaus for a time. In some areas, the plateau can become a slight decline, especially if the area is overheated and attracting never-before-seen prices. The stair pattern looks like the diagram in figure 2.1 (overleaf).

The rising lines in figure 2.1 indicate the years the property increased in value and the flat lines indicate the years when the property was stable. Depending on the property and the area, the graph will have a different appearance for properties in different areas.

Figure 2.1: stair-like pattern reflecting
increasing values of the property market

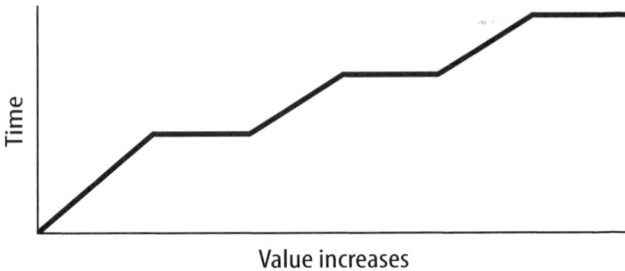

Rent returns usually behave differently. It is true that in some areas, rent returns can be affected by external forces pushing up demand. However, generally speaking, in well-established areas that are not subjected to a sudden external influence that changes the pattern, returns are linked to the CPI. That being the case, the line for rent increases is a far smoother one, and while it will never be entirely straight, it tends to have an upward trend. If we place the two lines together on a graph, then the result will look like the illustration in figure 2.2.

Figure 2.2: comparison of rental
returns and property values

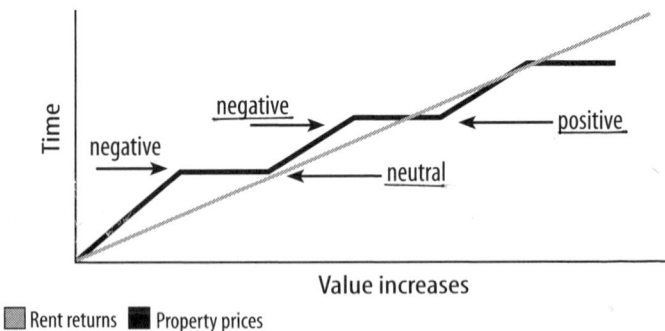

In figure 2.2, you can see that the arrows above the midline point to the times in the cycle when the property is likely to bring a negative cash flow. Anyone who buys a property at that time will find the rent return too low to close the gap between income and expenses, even with on-paper deductions (that is, positively geared). This will result in the investor incurring a negative cash flow.

Below the line, there are two types of arrows. One indicates the time when the return is neutral. Investors who buy in this part of the cycle are likely to cover costs and, if the property *also* has on-paper deductions, they will also probably exceed costs with the resulting tax breaks.

The second arrow indicates the times when the property has a positive return and, in some cases, if this gap is big enough, the return is positive even without the on-paper deductions. Any deductions will simply make the positive cash flow even greater.

There are a few things to note about this diagram. Firstly, the cycle will be different all over the country—a standard graph will not apply everywhere.

Secondly, if you buy when the returns are positive, then your returns should stay positive, because your actual return relates to the original purchase price, not the value at the time. If, however, you purchased a property that was in a positive phase of its cycle and you sold it to someone when it was in a negative phase, then while it would have been positive for you, it will be negative for the new owner.

My husband and I bought a property in 1996 for my mum and dad to live in. At the time, we paid $190 000 for it and the market rent was $260 a week. Being new, it also had large on-paper deductions, so had we rented it out at the time we would have seen a good positive cash flow.

what are the on-paper deductions for new ones?

31

We sold the property three years later for $325 000. During that time, rents had only risen by the CPI value, or about 3 per cent a year. For the new owner, rent return would have been around $285 and even with the remaining on-paper deductions, this property would have struggled to return the purchaser a positive cash flow.

Choosing when to buy

The last thing to note is that you do not necessarily have to carry out complicated calculations and draw complex graphs for a property you are thinking of purchasing in order to establish where in the cycle the property is. No two cycles are the same, nor are they exact or regular. All you need to know is that, prior to purchase, the property is in its positive return part of the cycle, as this will forevermore affect your ability to realise a positive cash flow.

The purpose of outlining the mechanics of this graph at all is to show you that the country is certainly *not* running out of positive cash flow property. If you have researched an area and rejected it because it could not give you a positive cash flow, you should repeatedly go back in future months and years and see what the situation is at that time. Very often, an area you had found to have a negative cash flow a year or two ago will have a positive cash flow today.

I can't find positive cash flow property

I can look for positive cash flow property for four weeks and find nothing. Then, suddenly, in the fifth week there are six or more. Often, people look on the internet and when they can't find what they are looking for, simply believe that it cannot be found.

It takes not only time and patience to find positive cash flow property, but also perhaps a little bit of wheeling and dealing as well.

I already mentioned that a simple look will not necessarily reveal a positive cash flow property. While you can easily identify a positively geared property (because the rent return will be more than the expenses), determining if a property will provide a positive cash flow requires you to be able to make some assumptions, and then calculate the cash flow based on what you think the on-paper deductions will be. The calculator available as a free download when you buy this book will give you the tools to make those calculations.

However, there is still an extra step you need to take, and many people's ignorance of this step often means they can't find a positive cash flow, even when they use a calculator. The following illustration explains my point.

Trudi has been looking for property for weeks and not found anything. She finds a property with a purchase price of $145 000, and a rent return of $180 a week. When she does her calculations, this is what she discovers:

- rent return totals $9360 a year

- interest (at 7 per cent) is $10 640 (assuming $7000 was added to the loan for purchase costs)

- other costs to maintain the property are $2200 per year

- total outgo is $12 840

- the property has a negative cash flow of $3480 gross

- after her tax refund of $1044 (at the 30 per cent tax rate), her commitment would be $2436.

33

> Trudi uses the calculator in Destiny® FinSoft and works out that she would also have on-paper deductions of $6400 in year one. As she is in the 30 per cent tax bracket, this deduction gives her an additional $1920 back in tax. Her personal commitment is now reduced to $516 a year, or $9.92 a week.

What so many people fail to realise is that the 'purchase price' is actually an 'asking price', and the rent return is the 'current' return. Let us have a look at what might happen to this property with a bit of negotiation.

Negotiating

As soon as the current lease is up on properties I have just purchased, I almost always increase the rents by $5 a week. I have found that people rarely move out over an extra $5 and, in many cases, that the current rent has not been changed for sometime. Sometimes, once settled, I can make an even greater change to the rent return.

Where the property is not yet rented, I would still add $5 a week to the amount suggested by the property manager. So, how would this affect Trudi if she considered the rent return at $185 a week instead?

- income would increase by $5 a week to $9620
- raw loss is reduced by $260 a year down to $3220
- tax refund is reduced down to $966
- Trudi's commitment before on-paper deductions is now $2254, and after deductions is $334, or $6.42 a week.

Okay, so we are still in negative cash flow. Let's take a look at the price. What would the effect be if Trudi also negotiated $10 000 off the asking price?

- interest would reduce to $9940
- shortfall would be $2520 gross
- tax refund on this loss is $756 making the new raw loss $1764
- her on-paper deductions give her a further $1920 as a tax refund.
- she now has a positive cash flow of $156 a year.

Now when Trudi looks on the internet for properties, her calculations include juggling the rent returns and the purchase prices to see how low she would need to go to realise a positive cash flow. She can then make these low offers and hopefully find someone who is willing to take a little less on his or her property.

Summary

- Be careful that you do not let your personal feelings, or those of anyone you speak to, interfere with the chances of purchasing a viable property.

- Demographics change dramatically over time and 'yuck' areas of years ago often become the trendy areas of today.

- Economic vibrancy is the key to an area with every chance of growth.

- You don't need to *know* the area to consider a purchase there. By the time you have carried out your research, you will know the area, probably better than the locals who live there.

- The best opportunities for you are most likely to be in an area other than that in which you live. If you continue to simply choose to buy from your surrounding area, then you are putting all of your eggs into the one basket.

- Areas come into and out of positive cash flow all of the time. Never completely reject an area as viable for cash flow—always come back to it later.

- Consider slightly higher rents and lower purchase prices when looking for positive cash flow property.

Conclusion

How many times have you met someone who bought property in areas no-one else would touch and then, years later, made a large sum of money from its sale? On meeting them, usually you think, 'Why can't *I* be that clever?' The reason most people aren't is that they are unwilling to think outside the box and are very often frightened of doing something to which other people may not give their stamp of approval.

Reuben and I have always ignored public opinion and gone with what we thought was right based on our considerable research, and what history has taught us about the way property behaves. Most people wouldn't dream of investing where we choose to and yet, so far, the properties we have bought have all had at least an acceptable level of performance. Some have not been as good as others in terms of growth, but others have been phenomenal, and all of them have given us a positive cash flow. Yes, we have our share of tenant problems and property manager hassles, but I would venture to say that choosing the type of property we choose has not led to a higher incidence of any of these issues. In fact, we know people with property in far more 'trendy' areas, with large negative cash flow, who have suffered problems just like ours, so I think we are pretty normal.

Chapter 3

The boom and the bust — fact or fiction?

_____

Listening to the 'experts'

2005 was widely reported to be the year of the 'property bust'. The CEO of a national non-bank lender warned people not to buy property, as the worst was yet to come. Reporters wrote of huge impending losses for real estate investors, as state laws and rising interest rates were predicted to have a huge impact on property returns.

My husband and I, with our usual scorn towards scaremongering, took this as a great sign and dove headlong into more investing, buying 10 properties in the period from September 2004 to October 2005. Each and every one of these properties rose in value in that time by at least 10 per cent, with four of them rising over 15 per cent and one rising 25 per cent.

The problem with the reports is that they were all too subjective. For reasons beyond my comprehension, reporters and the like seem to think that the 'property market' means Sydney or Melbourne property. And yes, 2005 was not a good year for

Sydney, with losses in value of around 7 per cent, or Melbourne, where property stagnated, with small losses reported in a few areas.

But who said we had to buy in Sydney or Melbourne? While these cities suffered this battering, Adelaide was increasing by more than 10 per cent, Darwin by more than 12 per cent and Perth by well over 30 per cent.

I know I keep harking back to it, but there goes the herd mentality again—follow what everyone else is doing. And in this case, they could not have been more wrong. Yes, there was a property lull in Sydney and Melbourne (although personally, I see that as an opportunity to get a bargain rather than a time to stop looking), but at the same time, a great number of areas in this country were just starting the first boom they had seen for many years, and a little careful research may have helped you ascertain beforehand just where those areas were.

You are always so lucky!

In early 2004, we purchased a few properties—among them was one in Darwin, one in a suburb of Perth and one in south-east Brisbane. At the time, I was co-host of a local radio real estate show, where I talked about these purchases. Many people phoned in concerned that I had chosen to buy in 'far-flung' areas and wondering at my reasoning.

Some six months later, several articles were written by numerous journalists and, interestingly enough, these three areas were touted as being the next 'hot spots'. Six months after that, we had each of these properties re-valued, discovering a growth of 33 per cent on the Perth property, 27 per cent on the Darwin property and 15 per cent on the Brisbane property. Each one has since continued to grow.

My radio co-host commented at the time that he thought I was perhaps the luckiest investor he had ever met. 'How do you consistently pick the areas that someone ends up writing about six months later?' he asked.

Let me make it very clear that luck has very little to do with it. While I do understand that bad luck can strike anyone at any time, and I know that the power of positive thinking can go only so far when the odds seem to be against you, I also know that there are many ways to maximise the chances of success with property investing.

Become an emotional desert

Go to any seminar on property investing and you will undoubtedly hear that property investing is 'all about the numbers'. Generally, they say that if the figures stack up, then that is all that matters.

Neil Jenman, whose opinion I greatly value, would tell us otherwise, claiming that using your heart has a place in property investing.

I believe true success lies somewhere in between these two extremes. I have seen many, many properties, with great after-tax cash flows, that I would not touch with a 10-foot pole. Just because a property has a positive cash flow or a great rent return does not mean that it is worth buying, or that it will achieve your goals for future financial security. I have seen countless unfortunate investors become carried away by the glossy brochures handed to them at property and money shows. Lured by the promise of magnificent returns on attractive property, the unwitting investors are left high and dry when the returns simply do not materialise and they find themselves with a white elephant on their hands. On the other hand, I have met people who have allowed their emotions to influence their purchase decisions. They fall in love with a property—perhaps because they can see themselves living in it or have the plan of one day moving into it themselves—but then also suffer financial disaster because they didn't do any real research.

I remember seeing a television interview with a fairly prominent author who has written a few financial books based on her personal experiences. Asked to share her best tips for buying an investment property, she espoused the importance of taking a stapler with you when looking at property (to compile the loads of paperwork sales agents will hand you), ensuring you bring a magnet with you to test that the window frames are all real metal, taking your binoculars along to make sure the gutters were straight, and lastly, wearing your glasses to hide your emotions from the agent. Advice such as this may be useful once you reach the 'micro' level of property selection (for example, choosing between two potential properties), but there is much more important work to be done before you get to this point.

Buying property as an investment is about economic vibrancy first, and physicality second. Limiting your search criteria to the property itself will not bring you close enough to the real story to make a viable decision about property. And the only way we can get serious about buying a property in an area that satisfies the important criteria for economic vibrancy is to take your emotional hat off and put your analytical one on.

Become experienced at buying without looking

As previously mentioned, you must accept that good opportunities exist all over the country, and that a sound, well-performing portfolio will include a wide spread of property from many different areas. To do this, you cannot possibly hope to visit each and every opportunity, so you must become experienced at buying without needing to view the properties personally.

Again, this concept worries many people. They are concerned that they will buy property that has some serious defect or is in a 'bad' area, or is, simply, 'not very nice'. Other than that, there are no other legitimate reasons that I can imagine that make it necessary to view a property. It is unlikely that looking at it will change its outcome as an investment, as long as you have asked the 20 must-ask questions (chapter 3, *A Pocket Guide to Investing in Positive Cash Flow Property*) about every property you are considering.

For those too scared to take the plunge and buy without seeing, consider the following points.

Collecting data

The 20 questions will narrow down important information, such as vacancy rates, future development plans for the area and the general economic health of the city or town you are considering. Looking at a property will not tell you any of this.

Ensuring structural soundness

Pest and building inspections are designed to uncover any serious faults or defects in a property. Even if you view the property yourself, it is highly unlikely that you will be able to find flaws that a professional has overlooked. So, as long as you have these inspections done, the chances of you buying a property with a major fault are the same if you look as if you do not.

Assessing tenant needs

If you are buying property as an investor, chances are you own or are in the process of paying off your own home. You are a 'homeowner', not a renter. You may not be capable of choosing a property from the perspective of a 'renter', so when you view a property, you run the risk of rejecting real estate that may be perfectly acceptable rental accommodation.

Finding other eyes

I have discovered a little trick that gives me that extra level of comfort when I am considering buying a property I have not inspected. I phone a local property manager and explain that I am thinking of purchasing a particular property, and tell them that, in the event of me buying it, I would like them to manage it. I ask if they would mind sending someone out to take a quick look at the property to ensure that its general condition is okay, that it is not in an area known for its high crime element and that it appears to be 'rentable'.

Property managers generally know more about these things than you do, and if one is willing to do this on your behalf, they also deserve the job of managing the property if you do go ahead and make the purchase.

Local knowledge

Be very careful who you take advice from. A while back, a client of Destiny® was looking at buying property in Mount Isa. He had carefully carried out his research to determine his target group, and picked a property that he felt satisfied the rental demand for the area. He chose a block of four one-bedroom units. They were neat and tidy and had small courtyards, and were well suited to the needs of the town's itinerant miners, who wanted a place to sleep but not much upkeep responsibility. Upon having his contracts sent over to the recommended solicitor for conveyancing, he received a telephone call from the solicitor himself.

'Clearly, you are not a local,' the solicitor surmised.

'Well, no. I am from Sydney,' my client responded. 'Why do you ask?'

'If you were a local,' the solicitor replied, 'you would not be buying in that area!'

At this, our client phoned me in a panic and asked if I thought he should pull out of the deal.

I asked my client what had led him to choose that property. He explained that his research had uncovered a developing area with many new services planned and a high demand for rental accommodation. I asked him who he had targeted as his tenant base, and he told me that he thought miners made up the bulk of the renting population. I then asked him if he had planned to ever attract solicitors as tenants and, indeed, if he thought that solicitors generally rented at all in that area, and he said, 'No'.

'So, you are taking advice from someone who seems to know a lot less than you about the area, and who is part of a demographic that would not be consumers of your product anyway?' I noted.

My client sheepishly conceded the point and went ahead with his plans.

This is a very common story and it is crucial that you understand that locals will usually be able to tell you the best place to live in an area, but not necessarily the best place to invest.

The need to view

Looking at an abundance of pictures of a potential property is almost the same as viewing it in person. Last year, a friend of mine decided that she and her husband were going to buy an investment property, and had been seeking the rather subjective advice of well-meaning friends and family for their input.

My friend was aware that she didn't need to actually view the properties she was considering, but due to the absolute need she had to still get a 'feel' for her potential purchases, she would ask the agents selling the properties to send her copious pictures of the properties from every angle possible.

On this basis, she rejected a number of properties that seemed, to me at least, to satisfy some of the more important qualities of a viable investment property. Not wanting to see these opportunities go to waste, I forwarded the details to some clients who went ahead with the purchases.

Interestingly enough, each of these purchases have done well—they are fully occupied and growing in value. The property eventually chosen by my friend, which was, I admit, divine to look at, has fetched a lower return than she had hoped and, due to the premium price she ended up paying, has not grown in value as she would have liked.

The moral of the story? Viewing a property really does not change its ability to perform well for you as an investment. Exhaustive research is the only way we can ever maximise investing success, and this is something you can do from the comfort of your very own home.

The property cycle—truth revealed

How many times have you heard it claimed that property doubles in value every 10 years? People plan their entire retirement strategy on this claim, which is often spouted at so many seminars, usually conducted by salespeople spruiking their wares and giving false hope to people who are afraid for their financial futures.

To understand how the 10-year concept translates in real life, consider the following:

They claim that in England, property has doubled in value every 10 years since 1088. If this were true, then today there is not enough money in all the world to buy a block of land.

Let's look at this from a more local perspective. If you had come in on the first fleet and paid £1 for a block of land, today it would be worth around £7 522 000 (about A$18 million).

Having said that, there have been times in history where property values have indeed doubled in a 10-year period and other times where the doubling has occurred within shorter periods. In Australia, the years from the 1960s to the late 1980s were very good to anyone who purchased property, as housing affordability was at an all-time high, land was plentiful and people were living a much-enhanced lifestyle. The main point to note, though, is that it is definitely not a given that property will double every 10 years, and it certainly has not always doubled every 10 years. At any time, property can experience a sustained period of stability and at other times it can be subject to losses, although in the main these are not usually great losses.

In order to double every 10 years, property has to grow by more than 7 per cent per year, every year. While this certainly does happen to some properties, there is an equal number of properties that will grow far more slowly than that, in both the city and the country. And when a few periods of no growth or negative growth occur, the bottom line is compounded. Take a look at the two examples overleaf.

In the second example, growth was good for eight years, stable for one year and a small loss was incurred for one year; however, the final figure was almost 20 per cent less than the figure in the first example. Anyone planning on a retirement income from an assured doubling every 10 years may find that the true outcome is considerably less than anticipated. And, if you also used a negative gearing approach along the way, your ability to recoup the years of financial input may be severely reduced or eliminated altogether.

Example A	Example B
$100000 property value doubling in a 10-year period (7.2% growth per annum)	**$100000 property value, 7.2% growth each year with no growth (or loss) in year 4, and a 7% loss in year 8**
1 107 200	1 107 200
2 114 918	2 114 918
3 123 192	3 123 192
4 132 062	4 132 062
5 141 570	5 132 062
6 151 763	6 141 570
7 162 690	7 151 763
8 174 403	8 140 836
9 186 960	9 150 977
10 200 421	10 161 847

It is a mistake to plan for a property portfolio to double in 10 years, if this is how long you plan to own it. It is wishful thinking, and those who espouse this theory have probably chosen to highlight a few 10-year moments in time where this has actually happened, and ignored the many other times when property has stagnated and had a severe impact on the 10-year readings.

There are, however, two other facts about the property cycle that may help you to not only have reasonable expectations about your property, but to put together a stable portfolio with promise of considerable growth.

Cycle—yes, consistent—no!

It is true that property behaves in cycles. Demand for property comes in and out of vogue and the demographic make-up of any area will always have an impact on whether property is booming in that location, or not. The factors that can prompt a boom in an area include the following:

1. A scarcity of land for new buildings will put pressure on the prices of existing properties.

2. Large numbers of residents in the 35 to 50 year-old age group contribute to escalating values. It is between these ages that people become less likely to move to another area. By 35, people are usually already living in their second home, and this will be the home that they stay in to raise their children, enabling them to remain in the same schools and to build friendship networks of their own. When this happens, there will be fewer sales and so more demand on any sales that occur. More demand than supply will always equal growth. Of course, the reverse is also true, and in areas where people have children already grown up and they are approaching retirement, we will see more sales and more supply, and therefore a slowing down of prices.

3. Future development plans by the council will most definitely result in price increases, particularly if this development involves additional services or beautification.

4. A boom in a large town or city most often echoes, becoming a boom a year or two later in surrounding areas that are suitably supported by services of their own.

5. An increase in the number of small businesses opening and a decrease in the commercial vacancy rates will contribute to the growth in residential property values.

6. A <u>sustained population growth</u> will create demand that prompts a rise in values.

7. A <u>diversity of industry</u> will result in population growth and a related values increase.

The not-so-certain selling points

Equally, you must be very careful about the following factors, which are often used as marketing tools by salespeople trying to sell property. These points, though based on truth, may be subjective or temporary and so may result in short-term, yet unsustainable, price increases.

1. *<u>Population and/or occupancy figures quoted from seasonal studies</u>*—many areas boom in summer and lull in winter and clever marketers use figures quoted from the high season, ignoring those from the low season.

2. *The promise of a future, <u>unconfirmed event</u>*—such as a new airport or a new casino.

3. *The advent of a major new contract for the main industry in town*—this does not guarantee that industry will still be around to fulfil that contract.

4. *<u>A recent large boom that has now flattened</u>*—I spoke to a reporter not long ago about the large boom that occurred in Bunbury, WA, in 2005. She asked me, 'So, should we all run off to Bunbury to buy then?' I replied, 'No, it's too late. The boom has happened and is now over, for the time being. It would be far better to find somewhere like Bunbury that hasn't boomed yet.'

Watch and wait

Knowing that property booms in cycles that may even be predictable is one thing, but as I mentioned in chapter 2, it is important to note that it doesn't behave in the same cycle all over the country. When we are being advised to hold back until a better time, we must know that this simply means to hold back in the area being reported on. It doesn't mean that it is necessary to hold off buying altogether. And it also means to watch the 'lulling' area very closely for signs that it is ending, so that you can buy a bargain (as long as it is positive cash flow) at the bottom of this cycle.

The *real* 10-year theory

We have now established that the 10-year cycle may not mean that property doubles every 10 years. In my own fairly conservative approach, I prefer to consider that property increases by half its value (or around 4 per cent per annum) in a 10-year period. This way, I am more likely to underestimate, probably considerably, the real end value of my property, as the past years have shown me that a figure somewhere in between—that is, 6 per cent—is more than likely to be correct.

Reuben and I have been buying property for almost nine years now. The majority of the property we have purchased has been bought in the past three years—it was 18 months between purchases number one and two, another year until number three, a year again for number four, and once we got to the six-year mark, we started to become more aggressive. This is a likely scenario for most people, and later in this book I will explore that further.

The total purchase prices of our properties is $3 897 000. Their collective value today over $6 million. This represents a growth of around 50 per cent across the entire portfolio and takes into consideration the fact that some of these properties had, at the time of writing, only been held for 12 months.

However, I must point out that some of our properties have done really well and some have done not so well. We purchased

[handwritten margin notes: 1, - 18 months -, 2, - 12 months -, 3, - 12 months -, 4, more aggressive]

property in Cairns in 1997 for $161 000. In 2002, it was valued at $145 000 (more due to the fact that we paid too much to a clever marketer, and I believe that $145 000 was probably its true market value at the time we purchased it). Today, almost nine years later, it is worth $200 000, which represents an average growth of only 2.5 per cent per annum. However, if you consider the growth since 2002, it has been about 8 per cent per annum, and, in fact, most of that growth happened in a two-year period, making it more than 17 per cent per annum for those two years.

This brings me to my next topic—my real 10-year theory. Having examined the progress of my own portfolio, and that of friends and clients, I believe that while property may not double every 10 years, in each 10-year period, providing you have done your research and chosen well, you should experience at least one boom period. And, during this boom period, you may get a large enough growth to make the 10-year cycle very profitable.

Since you cannot know whether your boom will come in year 1, year 5 or year 10, then you must be prepared to adopt a 'buy and hold' strategy for a period of at least 10 years. Selling before that time could well mean that you miss the boom and so do not maximise your returns.

Further, since the cycle of property happens differently all over the country, you must also be prepared to buy widely. Imagine if you bought all of your property in one area, and the boom for that area did not happen until year 10? The way to build a substantial portfolio is to use growing equity to leverage into more property. If your growth does not come until year 10, by then prices everywhere will have increased and your ability to leverage from this growth will be more limited.

If, on the other hand, you buy property all over Australia, at any one time something in your portfolio will probably be booming.

If this is the case, you will be experiencing consistent growth and increasing your ability to leverage into more and more property, while they are still affordable.

Summary

* Property behaves in cycles, but not the same cycle all over the country.

* You must learn how to make choices about property that do not involve your feelings—few of us have a gut-feeling where property is concerned and any feelings we do have will simply relate to the physical appearance of the property.

* You do not need to physically view a property to know if it is a good investment or not—often, viewing it may lead to you rejecting what could be a good option.

* It is a myth that property doubles in value every 10 years. Some properties do, but many do not.

* In a 10-year cycle there will probably be at least one *do not sell* period of good growth in all well-chosen properties. *before this boom!*

Conclusion

We have found that, because we choose to spread the areas in which we buy all around the country, our portfolio as a whole does very nicely. And because we choose to utilise positive cash flow rather than negative gearing, we have been able to buy more properties, and therefore we have been able to spread our investments even more and access more opportunities. The performance of the whole makes up for any problems or lack of performance of any one property, and this is the beauty of buying lower priced, good growth, positive cash flow property.

Chapter 4 _____

Cash flow or growth
— why not both?

_____

Do you have to choose?

In 2004, I attended a major property show at which I and several other people were keynote speakers. Since I believe that you can learn something new every day, I always try to sit in on other speakers' presentations and this way I often pick up some new information or reference material to help me with my own investing.

I was a bit alarmed, however, to hear one speaker (and advocate of inner-city property investing) ask the question, 'Would you rather have property that gives you a positive cash flow, or property that grows over time?' This speaker then went on to compare a portfolio of $1 million worth of property with a $250 a week positive cash flow ($130 000 over 10 years) to a portfolio of inner-city properties with the infamous 'doubling' over 10 years. The latter provided a gross profit of $1 million, or a net of $870 000 after the input of $250 a week (the negative gearing loss).

This terribly simplistic view overlooked so many important points. Firstly, it failed to recognise that the $250 a week on the positive cash flow property would repay debt, minimise interest (and so increase the $130 000 considerably as less interest is paid) and allow for additional leveraging as equity is created. This would allow the investor to buy more property, thereby gaining more exposure, while the negative gearing investor, despite the gains, would probably not be able to afford to buy any more.

More importantly, this speaker was asserting that, when investing in property, you had to choose between cash flow and growth—and, in doing so, made the assumption that you could not have both!

I am not sure where the information for this assertion was sourced, but this attitude is very typical of that of most people who think gaining a positive cash flow is all about buying cheap properties in isolated areas with no hope of growth in the foreseeable future.

Having your cake

My own experience, and that of many of my readers, has proven that, careful research and choosing can mean that you buy property in areas that not only experience booms but also that sometimes experience booms larger than many capital cities. Let's consider those investors who have been clever enough in recent times to buy in Ballarat, Bendigo, Airlie Beach, Noosa, Bunbury and many other areas just like them—solid properties, previously with a positive cash flow (before their respective booms, of course) which had stunning growth rates of up to 50 per cent. Try to tell them that opting for a positive cash flow meant that they bought properties with no growth potential.

This is not about having to choose between positive cash flow and growth. Some positive cash flow properties may not grow well, and some not at all, and, of course, you should try to avoid buying into areas with no indicators that there is a chance for growth. The flip side to that coin is that sometimes supposed 'blue-chip' property in expected growth areas does not perform as expected either. Many people who have invested in inner-city Sydney and Dockside in Melbourne have lost vast sums of money because they chose negatively geared, inner-city property that they thought would boom and make them a fortune. The playing field would actually seem pretty level in that respect, and to me it appears that you have as much chance of making a bad selection with a negatively geared property as you do with a positive cash flow one.

That said, let us look at a few examples of different kinds of portfolios, so that you can determine for yourself the one that is ultimately more appropriate for you.

Scenario 1

Mary earns $50000 a year and wants to buy blue-chip, presumably high growth property. The equity she has in her own home allows her to purchase two properties in the city valued at $300000 each, which both have a negative cash flow of $60 each per week. Her debt to buy these two properties is $620000, as she has $10000 costs on each.

This $60 each per week is her commitment after she has met all costs and claimed her tax break. Although Mary has chosen property with on-paper deductions, the choice of inner-city property meant that she received a lower percentage rent return as is often the case with higher priced, blue-chip property. Therefore, she has a real loss of $90 each a week (rent return less costs and loan interest) and for this receives a 30 per cent tax break, or $30.

This means that Mary's total commitment to these properties is $120 a week, and because of this she is unable to afford to buy any more than just two. In addition, this high commitment means that she cannot make extra repayments into her own home loan, nor can she make repayments other than interest repayments on her investment properties. Over time her rent returns do increase slightly in line with those of the CPI, however, so do her costs and she is still unable to find another $60 for a third property.

Mary holds these properties for 15 years. At that time, her position is as follows:

- If we assumed an 8 per cent per annum growth rate, her properties are worth $1 900 000. This is an optimistic forecast for this amount of time, however.

- At the end of this 15-year period, Mary's debt still sits at $620 000. This is because, as previously mentioned, she has only been able to make interest repayments and has not reduced the principal from its original amount.

- Her net worth (that is, the value of the investment property less the balance of her debt) is $1 280 000. Mary now has two choices. She can continue to hold the properties, and use the rent return as income. If we said rent return was 5 per cent (although city properties are usually less than this), then the properties would have a total gross rent of $95 000. However, she does not own these properties outright, because she has a debt. For the purpose of this exercise, we could say that Mary owns 68 per cent of the properties and the bank owns 32 per cent, so Mary would receive $64 600 of the rent as personal income. As an alternative, Mary could sell her entire portfolio and invest the net proceeds (after CGT) elsewhere.

- As Mary has had to pay $60 a week on each property, then in a sense she has invested $93 600 ($60 per week for 15 years) in order to receive this return.

This scenario looks quite good from here, and it appears that Mary's strategy has paid off and provided her with an opportunity to replace her current income and so leave the paid workforce. It must be pointed out that the $120-a-week forced savings did result in some sacrifices for Mary along the way and, at times, she was concerned that rising interest rates or vacancies would force her to sell earlier than anticipated.

As I have said previously in this book, if you can afford it, there is nothing wrong with this strategy. However, it does have limitations, and I would now like to show you how a positive cash flow strategy, with carefully chosen property, can deliver a better result than this scenario *even if* growth is considerably lower.

Scenario 2

Peter also has a $50 000-a-year income and also wants to invest in property. He decides to take an alternative route and buy property that gives him money in his pocket each week, that is, positive cash flow property. He seeks property in strong regional areas with good cash flows and every chance of growth due to the stability of the area.

He starts by buying one property valued at $150 000, with a positive cash flow of $20 per week. The property Peter buys has a higher relative rent return than the ones Mary bought — they are in a thriving town with some pressure on rents. The $20-a-week positive cash flow he receives, however, is his after-tax cash flow — his rent return, less his costs, less the on-paper deductions result in a tax break for Peter. This tax break not only makes up the shortfall between income and expenses, it gives him an extra $20 a week left over.

As Peter has no cash input (in fact, he has $20 a week more after he bought the property than he had prior), he buys another property for $150 000 every six months, each year. In reality, he probably could acquire property at a faster rate than this, but, for the purpose of this example, let's keep it fairly simple.

Peter holds these properties for 15 years. At that time, his position is as follows:

- If we considered a more conservative 5 per cent per annum growth, Peter has property valued at $6 800 000. This takes into account the fact that his last purchase was made six months prior and each purchase has increased in value by 5 per cent per annum, only for the period they have been owned.

- His total debt, considering $5000 worth of purchasing costs on each, was $4 650 000. However, Peter ensured that the $20 a week was channeled into this debt. This meant that his debt has been reduced by at least $235 000 (his total cash flow) to be, at most, $4 415 000.

- The net value (gross value less debt) of all property held is $2 400 000. Like Mary, Peter has two choices. He can continue to hold the properties, and use the rent return as income. If we said rent return was 5 per cent (although regional properties' returns are usually higher than this), the properties would have a total gross rent of $340 000. However, he does not own these properties outright, because he still has debt, albeit a reducing one, on the properties. In Peter's case, he owns 35 per cent of the properties and the bank owns 65 per cent, so Peter would receive $119 000 of the rent as personal income. If Peter continued to receive higher-than-city rent returns (say, even 6 per cent), then this figure would increase to $144 000 per annum and beyond. As an alternative, Peter could also sell and invest the net proceeds (after CGT) elsewhere.

- If Peter had experienced the same growth as Mary (8 per cent), his property would be worth $8 633 631 gross, $4 218 631 net and he would have a net income of $210 931 per year. If Mary saw the same growth as Peter (5 per cent), her portfolio would be worth $1 247 356 gross, $627 356 net and provide her with a yearly income of just $31 368.

- If Peter also used rapid mortgage reduction principles (that is, the right loan *and* a system, which is explained in detail in *How to Create an Income for Life*, chapter 9) he would increase this bottom line significantly as his debt would be considerably lower.

The results

From these illustrations, you can see that:

- At the end of the period, Peter has the potential to make almost double the income that Mary can, even with 38 per cent less growth.

- If they both experience the same rates of growth, Peter would still be considerably ahead.

- Peter had a cash flow built in to manage rising interest rates or vacancy risks, and so had more chance of being able to hold onto his property for the entire 15-year period. A change to interest rates or occupancy levels may have forced Mary to sell before the 15 years were over.

- Although Peter's property was cheaper and experienced a lower growth, he was able to buy more property and so gain a greater exposure to a growth market, even if that growth was lower.

You can play with the above scenarios as much as you like — allow Peter less property, even lower growth, or give Mary a better rent return — and still Peter's strategy will win hands down. In addition, Peter has enjoyed more personal security with the knowledge that he has bought property with a cash flow to manage risk, and in a price range that will make it easier to sell if needed.

All in one place or many?

Walk the halls of any property show or expo and I guarantee that you will spot several exhibitors sporting incredible models of the latest condos on offer in some stunning holiday location. Who can resist the temptation to gaze longingly at the little apartments depicted with tasteful finishings, choosing which one to buy and then sitting back to rake in the promised return?

Often, apartments such as these, or many of the house and land packages and other options on offer, come with hefty price tags. Generous growth projections can make these opportunities seem far more lucrative an offer than they really are.

I am frequently asked how much should be spent on any one property and, of course, as for all things, I have an opinion on that subject! However, I must say that mine is an opinion based on facts and research and a great deal of common sense.

If I had $600 000 to spend on property (or knew the bank would lend this amount to me) then I would far rather purchase four properties valued at $150 000 each than I would one at $600 000 or even two at $300 000. The reasons why are as follows.

There are more properties to choose from in this price range

current range : 200,000 – 300,000

If you do an Australia-wide property search on the internet and your search criteria is real estate within the $100 000 to $200 000 price range, then you will have a far greater number of results than you would in any other price bracket. Because of this, you will have a far greater choice and less likelihood of buying emotionally.

Some years ago, a client of mine had found a Queensland property she wanted to buy. She had tried to be unemotional, but still could not help but look at a couple of photographs on the internet. The property itself was unremarkable, in fact a perfect choice for a rental — easy care, no lawns, besser block walls, and one of many like it in the same area.

As the few bad apples are likely to do, the selling agent was secretly playing her off with another buyer and, even after my client had thought she had secured the property, this agent sold it to someone else.

My client rang me in tears to tell me that she had missed the property.

'Don't worry,' I soothed, 'there were at least four others just like it — buy one of them.'

'But I wanted *this* one,' she replied, unaware of her lack of logic and of how she had, after all, become emotionally involved.

When you have many to choose from, you have the luxury of being able to make low offers on several, hoping that one of these offers is taken up. Do be aware that *too* many available properties may mean an oversupply in the area; however, where buying and selling is highly active, being spoilt for choice means that you can have the upper hand.

There are more tenants available to rent lower priced properties

In the main, lower priced properties with proportionately lower rents will attract more tenants. This is not to say you should be purchasing beaten-up dives at bargain-basement prices so you can be a slum lord and rent out substandard accommodation. However, many properties in the $100000 to $200000 price range will be in large demand for rental. When one tenant moves out, another is often waiting to move in. This is not usually the case with properties demanding a higher rent return.

They can be easier to sell, and you can liquidate just part of the portfolio if the need arises

Buy one property at $600 000 and suddenly find yourself needing some cash, and you have to sell the whole thing. Buy four for the same total price, and in the event that you do need to realise some of your gain, you may only need to sell off part of your portfolio. As well as that, there are many more buyers in the lower third of the market than any other sector. <u>Lower priced property will sell in a much shorter period of time than more expensive ones.</u>

You can spread more effectively

One high priced property means that you have to have all of your eggs in the one basket. If the area you choose goes up in value, good for you — you have made a gain. If not, your entire investment has stagnated.

Buying many cheaper properties means that you can spread your investing all over the country. <u>You can buy one in each state if you like.</u> And when you do this, you will probably find that when one area is plateauing, another will be booming, and when the booming property begins to flatten out, the plateauing one may well then take off. You will have a greater chance of buying property that does really well if you can have a little piece of many markets.

You have greater chance of higher growth

For a $1 million property to increase by 10 per cent, it has to rise by $100 000. For a $100 000 property to increase by 10 per cent, it only has to increase by $10 000, and in some cases <u>a simple repaint, tidy up and new carpets can add at least this value.</u> It is much easier to gain higher percentage value price increases from lower priced property than it is from those in the higher price ranges.

As you can see, there are many sound, common-sense reasons for choosing low priced, well-placed, good cash flow property for your portfolio.

Summary

- Purchasing properties with a positive cash flow often means that you can buy more property, resulting in greater exposure and a higher ultimate net worth.

- Positive cash flow properties chosen well can still show excellent rates of growth.

- Low priced property is easier to buy as it is more abundant, and easier to sell as there are more buyers in that market.

- Lower priced property is also easier to tenant as there are more tenants in this market.

- You can spread a portfolio of lower priced property more easily than you can spread a portfolio of higher priced ones.

Conclusion

I hate the expression 'It's not rocket science', but you know, it's really not! I think that people try to make property investing too difficult — as if there is a complicated process to follow that can only be revealed by the very clever.

I also think one of the main problems most people have is worrying about what other people are going to think about them. It's all very nice to go a barbecue and rave to your friends about the gorgeous condo in Noosa you own. I have to admit, when I talk about the three flats in Krambach we bought (and which consequently rose in value by 50 per cent in 18 months and enjoy an exceptional positive cash flow), very few people have any real interest and the main comment I hear is, 'Where on earth is Krambach?'

Don't forget what I said about pioneers. Pioneers are usually pretty lonely people, because they are the first to map uncharted territory. So, forget what friends and relatives think of you, forget about the popular choice and steel yourself against the slick tongues of those suited marketeers bearing glossy brochures and dreams of romantic real estate. Instead, start to think about how you can wisely, and safely, begin your own portfolio and create a secure retirement income.

_____

Chapter 5

On the money
— getting the right loan

Money matters

Another way I could get rich would be to ask for a dollar every time someone asks me whether they should have an interest-only loan or pay principal and interest on an investment debt. Knowing how to borrow well and structure effectively is one of the most misunderstood steps in the investment process, second only, of course, to obtaining positive cash flow!

Last year I was at the home of a great friend of mine who also happens to be one of the most respected financial advisers in the country. There were a number of other people from the financial services industry in attendance and at one point, the conversation turned to this very topic.

Our host commented that it is always better to pay the 'interest only' on your investment loans, and any extra cash you have should be invested elsewhere to make a gain. His theory revolved around the fact that home loan rates are only around 7 per cent (and so repaying principal essentially means that you are earning 7 per cent on your money), whereas, invested elsewhere, your money could probably attract higher rates than this.

'What about the fact that when you repay principal you gain equity, and when you gain equity you can leverage again, sooner, while property is still at a lower price?' I asked him. 'That way, your money is not only earning the 7 per cent interest you save, it is also earning whatever growth rate you can get on the money that has essentially been put back into a growth market?'

With that, everyone else in the room said, 'Yes, what about that?'

He had to concur with my reasoning and admitted that he hadn't quite looked at it that way before. If you add to that the concept that, if people *don't* make principal and interest repayments and instead keep the extra money for themselves, it is less likely to make it into another investment and more likely to end up spent somewhere, then I stand firmly behind the argument for principal and interest repayments. If you are smart enough to find and invest in positive cash flow property, and you find yourself with extra money left over each week, what better place for it to go than right back into the debt you have for that property?

Having said all this, it is not, of course, quite as simple as that, and setting up the right loan structure and then paying it off correctly is far more complex and deserves your attention.

What type of loan?

There are hundreds of different loan products on the market today, and choosing the right one can be like navigating a veritable minefield. When people ask me whether they should get a principal and interest (P&I) loan or an interest-only loan,

I usually tell them, 'Neither'. This question assumes that they are the only choices available, when in fact there is a third, more viable option, which is indeed my own preference.

You see, while I believe it is crucial that you pay principal and interest *somewhere* in your loan portfolio, a P&I loan does not give you the flexibility you need if you have decided to build a big portfolio. An interest-only loan does not give you the flexibility either, and has some drawbacks that I will go on to explain. However, the third option gives you the best of both worlds if you know how to use it well.

There is a complete chapter in *How to Create an Income for Life* (chapter 7) that goes into great detail about banks, borrowing, loan products and loan features. To gain a full understanding of borrowing, which is vital if you are to become a property investor, be sure to familiarise yourself with that chapter. For now, here is a summary of the major three loans that most people will consider for their investing, and an outline of the one that will work best for most investors.

Option 1—P&I (principal and interest) loan

A principal and interest loan requires regular, monthly repayments so that the entire loan, and all of its interest, can be paid off within a pre-agreed period, which is usually 25 or 30 years. As the interest rate on a loan such as this will usually be 'variable' (that is, it fluctuates as the Reserve Bank rates change), the actual repayments made will alter each time there is an interest rate change, so that the loan can still be repaid in the required period.

A principal and interest loan will have a variety of features depending on the bank or lender used. These may include:

- a discount off the variable rate for the life of the loan

- portability, so that you can transfer it between properties

- the flexibility to make extra repayments, or fortnightly and weekly repayments, which will reduce the term

- the ability to draw back (or 'redraw') any 'additional' repayment of the principal that you have made over and above the agreed principal reduction

- the ability to 'fix' the rate for an agreed period during the term of the loan

- giveaways to attract you to the product, such as free holidays, petrol vouchers and discounted application fees.

While a loan such as this is highly suitable for people who wish to purchase an owner-occupied residence, there are also limitations on this type of loan that make it unsuitable for an investment purchase. They include:

- an inability to draw back to the full approved amount of the loan if you wish to use the equity gained in your property (from extra repayments) as a deposit on another property

- the inability to increase the loan—you have to get extra loans if you want more money

- a lack of flexibility—you cannot easily put money in and take money out as you can with other loans, and this reduces your ability to offset interest

- the ability to 'split' the loan to represent different purposes, which is a feature of other loan options, as you will see as you read on.

For those people who need a 'forced savings' type of option, a P&I loan may suit. Since you are required to make the agreed repayments and you cannot get back any of this money, then those who are not well-disciplined may find it necessary to use this type of loan. Having a loan such as this will ensure that, at the very least, you finalise the loan within the pre-agreed period.

However, for serious investors who know they can manage their money well and will not be tempted to access available funds if given the chance, option 3 will be more suitable.

Option 2 — interest-only loan

An interest-only loan requires a repayment equal to the interest that has accrued for that month. Generally, there will be an agreed term, typically around five to 10 years, during which your interest-only period applies, and during this time, you must make a monthly repayment that covers the interest and ensures that the principal remains the same — as the name suggests, you pay the interest only.

Most interest-only loans will have the same features and drawbacks as those listed above for a P&I loan.

If you have a P&I loan on your own home that you are yet to repay, an interest-only loan for your investment property may be a viable option for you.

When you buy a property as an investment, the interest on the debt is tax-deductible. (Later in this book I will look at this further.) Interest on the debt on your own home, however, is not tax-deductible. It makes no sense to make repayments that reduce the tax deductibility of your investment property (by having a P&I loan on an investment property) while you still have a balance remaining on your personal, non-tax-deductible debt. You should make interest-only repayments on your investment debt and put as much money as you can, including your surplus funds and the positive cash flow from your investment property, into repaying the personal debt first. (Again, this will be covered in detail later in this book.)

Having now looked at P&I loans and interest-only loans, let us explore the third option, which provides the benefits of both, without the drawbacks of either.

Option 3 — line of credit loan

There are dozens of line of credit options available from many different lenders today. It is vital that you understand that they are *not* all the same and not all of them will work well for you, personally.

Before taking on any loan product, be aware that borrowing is a very personal thing. What is right for you may not be right for your friends or for other investors, and so it is crucial that you have a true expert in both tax and property investing advise you on the best loan for you.

A line of credit is basically a mortgage loan with a 'limit' rather than a loan amount. While the limit you receive may be the same as the loan amount you would have had approved on a standard loan, it is the way you use this type of loan and the ongoing features that make it a much more viable option, rather than the fact that it is a line of credit.

In essence, you apply for a line of credit in the same way that you apply for any other loan — using a loan application and providing all of the documents required by the bank. Once you have had this loan approved, you are provided with a 'limit' that represents the loan amount. In most cases, the limit will be 80 per cent of the value of the property you own or are buying, unless you have applied for a loan with a higher 'loan to valuation ratio' (or LVR), and have paid the bank the required 'lender's mortgage insurance' (or LMI), which is an insurance premium to protect the bank. (This concept is covered later in this chapter.)

Once you have the loan in place, you may pay as much or as little into the loan by way of a repayment, whenever you like, as long as you meet the following two basic requirements:

1. You must at least pay off the interest that accrues and is charged to the account each month (therefore, there must be at least a monthly repayment).

2. You must ensure that the account never becomes overdrawn — that is, the approved limit is not exceeded — unless you have applied for an increase to this limit.

In a nutshell, subject to lending criteria (see chapter 7 of *How to Create an Income for Life* for a complete list of basic bank-lending criteria), you can borrow up to 80 per cent of the value of a property (or up to 90 per cent if you are prepared to pay lender's mortgage insurance) as a line of credit.

The reasons I like to use a line of credit loan are many, and include:

- A line of credit can be 'split' to represent different purposes and this can make your accounting much easier. For example, in my own portfolio I have just one loan, with one loan number. The amount of this loan is large and the security that the bank holds to advance this loan includes all of the property that I own. However, I have been able to 'split' this loan into different accounts, one that represents any personal borrowings I have (which are non-tax-deductible) and then additional accounts that represent the properties I own. At tax time, my accountant does not have to perform complicated calculations to ascertain the amount of interest I can claim as a tax deduction, as keeping the accounts separate like this means that I can simply apply all of the interest from one account to the property that it represents. Note that the sum total of all of the accounts may never go above the total limit of the loan; however, at any time, I can 'rearrange' the limits. For example, if one account has extra funds that I don't need for that property and another account on a property for which I may need some funds for a repair has no available funds, I can apply to the bank to make the extra funds available in the account I need it by reducing one and increasing the other. All of this makes tax accounting so much easier.

- When my properties have gone up a little in value and I have made some principal reductions to the loan by ensuring all of my positive cash flow is paid into the account, my loan will no longer be 80 per cent of the total values. At this point, I can have my properties 'revalued' and apply to have the overall limit of the loan increased back to 80 per cent. This will then make extra money available for another deposit on another property, which I can buy and add to the portfolio and so increase the loan further. Later, in chapter 8, there is an illustration from which you will be able to see how a portfolio grows through the combination of value increases, loan reduction and then loan increases.

- I can choose where I want to make principal reductions. Initially, it will be personal debt that is repaid first, and this will be done by placing all of my income from work and from rent and any other source I derive it, into the personal account of my line of credit. I then only ever draw back what I need for personal daily living expenses and leave everything else sitting in the loan, offsetting interest, until I need it (if at all). Once there is no personal debt left, I then begin to repay investment debt the same way, choosing one account to repay at a time.

- I can always get any extra repayments back as soon as I need them so I can freely place all excess money in the account, offsetting interest every day.

- If I were to sell a property and buy another in its place, I can freely 'substitute' the security without having to get a new loan and, therefore, without having to even apply for a loan at all. As long as the overall limit either stays the same or reduces (in the case of replacing one property with a cheaper one), then no loan applications need to be completed.

- I am able to keep the same loan forever, as the right line of credit will have no term. You see, since a line of credit is really a bank account with an overdraft limit, you need never have any other type of bank account except your credit card. This 'loan' becomes the place where you keep any money or savings you have and it can be operated like any other bank account — you can arrange direct debits and even have a cheque book. This is great as it means that, every time you buy or sell property, you do not have to discharge a loan and establish a new one — you just make the necessary adjustments to the one you have. I still have exactly the same loan I had when I bought my own home nine years ago — it is now much larger, there are many more properties securing it and it has many more accounts, but I still have the same loan number and all of my original direct debits are still in place.

Having a line of credit has made my investing life far more simple and my tax accountant's life far less complex. It has also meant that my accounting bills are a lot less expensive!

Apples and apples

Not all lines of credit are the same! In *How to Make Your Money Last as Long as You Do* I outline all of the features you must look out for in the line of credit being offered to you, and also the questions you should ask your bank manager about that bank's particular line of credit before you go ahead. Be sure that you read this and check your line of credit against this criteria. I have had literally hundreds of readers write to me to tell me that their line of credit simply does not perform for them and that they are sorry they ever got one — and, often, I find that they have a poor example of a line of credit.

Sometimes a line of credit may have a slightly higher interest rate than a standard variable loan, maybe up to 1 per cent higher. I still recall a client of ours from many years ago who was considering a line of credit that was a whole 2.5 per cent higher than what his current bank was offering him as a two-year special deal. <u>Our calculations showed that, even with the higher rate, he paid *less* interest overall because the flexible features of his line of credit allowed him to offset interest daily</u> by placing all of his money in the loan until he needed it. This was clear evidence that, if you know how to use your line of credit wisely, you can save a lot of interest and still have your money 'at call' in the event that you need it, even with a higher rate of interest.

The importance of discipline

Lastly, having a 'line of credit' is not a magic formula for your sudden success. The line of credit does not pay itself off more quickly and if all you ever do is put all of your money into it and take it all back out again, you will, in fact, be far worse off than you would be with a P&I loan. Lines of credit require great discipline and the ability to repay them quickly depends on ensuring that all of your cash flow, from property and from other personal income, is paid into the account and only your personal expenses are withdrawn. If you obtain a line of credit and then see it as an opportunity to get funds for holidays, cars and other things you normally would not buy, then you will not get ahead. You must have a systematic approach to how you pay off your debt and be sure that you have a strategy in place as well as a system by which you can easily track what you are doing regularly. *How to Create an Income for Life* outlines very important rules that must be followed if you are going to use a line of credit, so ensure you read them before proceeding with this type of loan.

Your friendly bank manager

Too many times I am told by clients that they simply cannot change their loan, or their bank, because their bank manager is such a nice person and has always done the right thing by them.

This is simply misplaced loyalty. The bank manager is *meant* to be nice to you—it is his or her job. I can assure you that once the longed-for promotion comes through, your bank manager is not going to decline it on the basis that you are a special client and you have been loyal to him or her!

In addition, I caution all investors to be very careful who they take advice from. Bank managers and almost all loan brokers are usually very good at their jobs and often have extensive knowledge about bank products. Very few of them know anything about tax and structure, however, and they are not qualified to give you advice about the best way to set up a loan. It is a fact that more than 90 per cent of the people who come through the doors of my company, Destiny® Financial Solutions, for property investing advice have either the wrong loan or the wrong loan structure, having followed the advice of a bank manager or broker. Once done, it can be very hard to undo and even harder to make retrospective claims on lost tax benefits.

Be very sure that you only ever take loan structure advice from someone who is actively involved in the property investment industry *and* who is qualified to give you financial and property investment advice.

Cross-collateralisation

At a recent seminar, a man in the audience told me that he always ensured that he went to a different bank for each loan. This meant that he had a lot of different loans with many different banks, which each held one or two security properties.

When I asked him why he wanted to make his life so complicated by having bits and pieces of everything all over the place, he responded, 'Because I don't want to be at the mercy of just one bank!'

'Oh,' I said. 'You would rather be at the mercy of many banks then?!'

In this country, when you borrow money you must pay it back. The bank holds collateral security in the form of property to ensure that, if you don't pay it back it has a way to recoup what you owe it. In the unlikely event that what you owe the bank exceeds what it can make by selling the security it holds, it will require you to find the money somewhere else. This can, and will, include you selling anything else you have in order to repay the bank in full.

It is a false notion that a bank only has the power to take the proceeds of security it directly holds. If you are found to have property elsewhere that may yield funds if sold, then you will be required to sell it, even if it is held by another bank. This means that there is no protection in having your properties held by many different banks, as your lender's power to recover monies due from you extends beyond the security it holds.

There are other disadvantages with having loans all over the place. Previously, I discussed the way a line of credit can be increased quite easily (subject to you satisfying basic lending criteria) once you gain equity in a loan and/or your property increases in value.

If each property you own is held by a different bank, then a single property must increase enough in value to generate a deposit to buy more property without having to re-mortgage the whole package or take some other complicated action. If, however, all securities are held with just one bank, then each property only needs a small increase in its value to make the total values enough to buy more through one simple loan increase. Here is an example to illustrate this.

Gary owns six properties mortgaged with six banks. Each property is valued at $150 000, and each loan is for $120 000.

There is a 6 per cent increase to all properties, making them each worth $159 000. Based on this, he could borrow an extra $7200 on each property, which would total $43 200.

Since his loans are with different banks, each bank will only give him an increase of $7200. While the total increase of $43 200 would be enough for a deposit on another property worth about $150 000 (considering his purchase costs), to make this equity available he will have to get either six additional loans from each of those banks, or re-do the whole package into new loans. The six additional loans will be messy and make tax accounting very difficult, and the new package will be costly, with discharges and re-registrations of mortgages, as well as loan stamp duties and all manner of other costs, involved.

Jackie, on the other hand, also owns six properties of the same value, all held with the one bank. She has a line of credit and it is divided into six sub-accounts, each of $120 000 and each representing one property.

Her properties also increase by 6 per cent, allowing her to borrow an extra $43 200. She sets this up as a seventh sub-account simply by applying for an increase to the loan. When she finds the new property (with, let's say, a value of $150 000), she will give this to the bank as extra security and then increase the amount of the seventh sub-account by a further $120 000. The total of this new sub-account, which is $163 200, is enough for Jackie to buy the property,

> pay all the costs and have some left over for ongoing costs, too. The entire process was quicker, cheaper and much easier than the path Gary had to take.

We call the process of giving all of your property to one bank in one group 'cross-collateralising'. Choosing not to cross-collateralise will *not* provide protection against having to sell more than what the bank holds in the event of difficulties. It will, however, make it harder for you to easily capitalise on the increasing values and more costly every time you need to adjust or increase your loan.

Capitalising interest

Some of you may remember a case some years ago where a 'mortgage reduction' company (that is, a group set up to advise people on how to pay off their mortgages quickly—very big in the 1990s, but almost non-existent in its original form today) gave advice to a couple who owned two properties, one an owner-occupied place of residence and one an investment property.

The loan set up for them was a line of credit with two accounts—one designated for personal debt (non-tax-deductible) and one for investment debt. The one for investment debt had a limit that was greater than the loan amount required. This is acceptable, since with a line of credit you only pay interest on what you use, and it can be useful to have some 'available limit' if there is enough equity, in case the property needs some repairs or otherwise.

The couple was then advised to pay all of their income and rents into the personal portion of the loan, and also draw personal expenses out of that portion too (so far, so good). They were also advised to draw all of the expenses for the investment property from this account (which is acceptable), but to make no payments to the investment portion at all, not even enough to cover the interest being charged to the account.

The result of this strategy was that the personal portion of the debt, which was receiving all of the payments, was being paid off very quickly, and the investment portion, which was receiving no repayments at all—not even interest repayments—was growing, creating a debt that accrued more interest every year (and so a greater tax deduction) and that threatened to be higher than the actual value of the property.

The couple claimed this increasing interest as a tax deduction and eventually the tax office took them to court for tax evasion. Initially, the couple was victorious; however, on the tax office's appeal, the original decision was overturned and the couple was ordered to repay the benefits they had claimed.

If you think about the basics of tax law for a moment, this process of the 'capitalisation' of interest was never going to be allowed. While you may claim interest on a debt used to purchase an income-producing property, and you may legally borrow more funds to carry out repairs, maintenance and renovations and claim the interest on that too, you may not make any tax claims on any item from which you derive a personal benefit.

In the above example, technically the capitalising interest was being used for personal benefit, since the funds that the couple should have used to make the interest repayments on the investment debt was actually repaying personal debt. There was a clear personal benefit to this strategy and that fact alone made it illegal.

It is certainly acceptable to divert all available funds, including your rents into your personal debt, and the tax office does not require you to make principal and interest repayments to your investment debt. It does, however, require that you at least meet the interest repayment on your investment debt. It also stipulates that any increase to this investment debt is only able to occur if you are using the funds for the acquisition of additional capital assets for the investment property or to carry out repairs and maintenance to an income-producing asset. If you are receiving any advice to the contrary, or someone suggests a scheme of repayment that sounds too good to be true, then it probably is! Take great care with any such advice before following it.

Mortgage reduction

In the late-80s, a clever scheme was invented that showed people how to pay off their mortgages more quickly. Essentially, it involved obtaining a line of credit and paying your income from all sources into this loan. To meet your expenses, you used a credit card with an interest-free period. At the end of each month, the credit card was paid off by drawing back some of the funds placed into the line of credit and then the process started again for the next month. By doing this, you were not only 'offsetting interest' by 'parking' all of the money you ever received into the loan (and so reducing the balance on which interest was accruing), if you budgeted well and ensured that your surplus funds stayed in the loan as extra repayments, then you also paid off your loan many years sooner than you otherwise would have if you were less prudent with your surplus income.

Whole companies were set up to tell everyone about the scheme and 'financial plans' were prepared for people to show mortgages repaid in one-third of the time, saving hundreds of thousands of dollars in interest.

What many of these early financial plans failed to accurately show was that the ability of the person to pay off the loan so early was not simply the result of having a line of credit and using a credit card, although this was certainly the thrust of the sales pitch. In order for the goal of early mortgage repayment as outlined in the financial plans to be achieved, consumers basically had to be sure that all funds over and above their budgeted expenses stayed permanently in the loan. Almost the same effect could have been achieved by making additional repayments to a standard loan, although the inflexibility of basic loans would have made using a 'rapid mortgage reduction' system almost too difficult. The other problem with almost all of these companies was that they charged very high fees simply for setting up the line of credit, and provided virtually nothing in the way of a system to ensure the goals were met, or support in the event that the consumer needed help to stay on, or get back on, the track.

Using a line of credit loan, attempting to offset interest in any way possible and making extra repayments to your loan is a prudent approach to owning your own home and to accelerating a property investment plan. Anyone with a loan should be prepared to invest all available monies, besides what they plan to allocate to personal expenses, back into his or her loan. My company, Destiny® Financial Solutions, promotes the use of this type of facility to those of our clients who are prepared to be committed and follow our system, and it has netted some great results for them.

The main problem back in the 80s and 90s was that many of these companies made it all seem as though it was magic, as if having the line of credit alone would result in rapid loan repayment. If all you ever did was deposit all of your money and then draw it all back out again (leaving only an amount equal to a loan repayment), the interest offsetting effect would only save a few years. While this is certainly better than doing nothing, you would save not nearly the number of years claimed by some of the 'plans' prepared for people.

Nowadays, it is against the law to compare the use of a line of credit to a standard P&I loan unless it is clearly stated how the line of credit is to be used and that, essentially, more than a standard repayment would need to be made to achieve great results. We caution all of our clients that, while a line of credit is by far the most flexible option and provides an excellent vehicle for rapid mortgage reduction and property investment, their success will depend more on effective money management and the commitment to using the strategy tracking tools we supply them, rather than the features of the loan itself.

The point to be taken here is that a line of credit gives you the opportunity to make great results happen where a standard P&I loan will not. The ability to 'park' money, knowing it is available to use if necessary, allows the flexibility to pay off your loan many years sooner.

Mortgage reduction — personal and investment debt

I am beginning to believe that there are many accountants who get short summaries of new tax rules and then try to apply them to their clients without fully understanding them. Certainly, in the Destiny® offices we get many, many people who are following advice from their accountants that is only 'half' right and that is costing them money, as well as the benefits that they could be receiving.

Some time ago, lines of credit being used to buy investment properties came under the watchful eye of the tax office. At the time, these facilities were considerably new and underdeveloped, and only a few options were available from a small number of lenders.

Those who were using them for investment purposes had generally refinanced their home loan and obtained an investment loan, all as a single line of credit. This single line of credit then had rapid mortgage reduction principles applied — all income and rents were deposited, a credit card was used for expenses and then, each month, a drawing was made to pay off the credit card.

As I have already explained, since interest on a personal debt is not tax-deductible, you are only allowed to make claims for the interest on any debt used strictly for investment purposes. When tax time arrived for people with a single, dual-purpose line of credit, it became incredibly difficult to calculate which part of the interest was truly for investment purposes and which part was personal use.

To do so, an accountant was usually needed to backtrack and calculate exactly how much interest had been charged on bona fide investment debt and expenses, and how much had been charged on personal debt and expenses, so that only that portion of the interest attributable to the investment debt could be claimed. This was an almost impossible task, and many accountants simply used the original formula that had applied to the original debt — for example, if originally the debt was attributed with 40 per cent applying to the personal portion of the debt, and 60 per cent applying to the investment portion of the debt, they would claim 60 per cent of the total interest accrued as an investment tax deduction.

The tax office took a different view, saying that if one single line of credit was used for both personal and investment debt, all deposits (that is, all income and rents paid into the account) would be treated as repayments of the principal as per the original formula (so for the previous example, each deposit would have 60 per cent allocated to the investment debt and 40 per cent allocated to the personal debt). All re-drawings, however, with the exception of those for yearly property costs, would be considered personal due to having been drawn back from the personal portion rather than having had the same

60/40 formula applied. This meant that the investment debt was always receiving a repayment (often larger than that being made to the personal debt), but nothing was ever being drawn back out. The personal debt was receiving repayments, but also suffering from all the re-draws. Very quickly, the investment debt would be repaid and the personal debt would, in fact, increase.

The advice from the tax office, and then many accountants, was to not use a line of credit at all if you had investment properties and you wanted to undertake a rapid mortgage reduction plan. As a result of this, many of our clients are now telling us that their accountant has advised them not to use a line of credit where some or all of the debt is for investment purposes.

This is another untruth that has come about simply because of the messy history of lines of credit. In fact, you can use a line of credit for your investing, but it is crucial that you ensure that the line of credit you do use allows you to separate, or split off, the loan that represents your personal debt from that which represents your investment debt. This way, you can direct all funds (income and rents) into the personal portion of this debt (if you have one), and as long as you ensure that a monthly transfer is made into the investment portion of the debt that represents all of the interest accrued for that month, you remain within the boundaries of tax law. Then, when tax time arrives, you may claim all of the interest accrued on the investment portion of the debt as a tax deduction, as you have kept it all very clean and easy to account for.

Mortgage reduction — investment debt only

Once you have finalised your personal debt, you may want to adopt a rapid mortgage reduction plan for your investment debt. Earlier, we established that, unless you have another investment plan to which you are prepared to commit, placing your excess funds and property cash flow into your investment debt is probably the best plan of action. True, it does reduce the amount of interest you can claim as a tax deduction, but the amount of lost tax deductibility pales in comparison to the extra leverage you can obtain through increased property investing. Note the following simple example.

Kate is in the 30 per cent tax bracket. She reduces her investment debt balance by $15 000 per year by directing all of her available funds into her investment debt, and only drawing back out what she needs to meet daily living expenses. After two-and-a-half years, she has reduced the balance of her investment loan and has enough equity, even without market growth, to buy another property valued at $150 000.

If this new property was to then grow at 6 per cent per annum, Kate would gain an extra $9000 in personal net worth (growth) from buying it.

At a 7 per cent per annum interest rate, this extra $15 000 per year that Kate leaves sitting in her investment loan has resulted in her paying $1050 per annum less in interest (which, in essence, is a further investment into this portfolio, as saving interest is the same as earning interest). This reduction in interest charges results in $315 a year in lost tax deductions.

So, Kate is paying $315 a year to gain $9000 in increased assets plus $1050 in loan equity, which, for those who like figures, is about a 3000 per cent return! (This does not include the fact that the interest saved is contributing to the next property purchase and that the principal reduction from leaving the $15 000 a year in the investment debt is continually buying her more equity and increasing her personal net worth.)

A word of caution

Having told you that this is the best way to use your cash flow, I would also like to issue a word of warning—the tax office does not like people who only have investment debt channelling their personal funds through their investment debt. If you do this, the tax office will assume that all deposits made to the debt are reducing principal, and that any subsequent drawings are *creating* a personal debt. It will not consider that you may be 'lending' your debt some personal funds to offset interest for a time, funds that you then wish to later take back. The situation may become one where you pay off investment debt in double-quick time and, in the process, create an unwanted personal, non-tax-deductible debt.

what?! .

To avoid this, there is a way that you can structure any investment debt you have to enable you to still use rapid mortgage reduction, but it is very complicated and requires a deep understanding of how the process will operate. Basically, the technique requires you to structure your loan in such a way that you split your investment debt into two accounts, with one of them having only a small limit. You then channel your deposits through this smaller account and each time the account's balance has been reduced to nil (as you have used rapid mortgage reduction), you should draw it to its limit by transferring a lump sum across to the second account (essentially making a lump sum, principal repayment). The small amount of interest you sacrifice by creating this small operating account (say, around $200 a year) is worth it for the benefits you then have of using rapid mortgage reduction.

How to Maximise Your Property Portfolio (chapter 9) does give more details on how this is to be done; however, many people are still unsure of how to put the structure in place. Setting up a structure such as this can be complicated and very difficult to understand, and you will need a professional to guide you and ensure it has been done correctly. Please be aware that obtaining and structuring a loan such as this is a service offered, at no cost to you, through any of the Destiny® branches.

Purpose and security

Ah, now we come to a topic that never fails to generate more confusion and bad advice! I can't believe that, with all that we now know about tax and with all of the test cases that have been reported in the press, there are still people receiving bad advice about what you can and cannot claim.

Two recent stories come quickly to mind. The first is that of a lovely, very trusting, client who had purchased a property in Cairns as an investment. She had used the new investment property and her own home as security for the borrowings, and her accountant had suggested she borrow $20 000 more than she needed for the property, so that she could buy herself a new car. He then claimed the interest on the entire debt as a tax deduction.

The second story is about a client who had an investment debt and a personal debt, kept nicely separate. The investment debt had been used to buy an investment property *and* $70 000 worth of shares. He was advised to sell off the shares and pay the $70 000 proceeds into his personal debt (which finalised it) but to keep claiming the interest on the entire investment debt (which included the $70 000 for the now non-existent shares), since it was 'secured' by the investment property.

The ability to make a tax claim for an incurred expense depends entirely on what the expense has been incurred for. If you have incurred the expense because you have used the money to purchase, repair, renovate or maintain an income-producing asset, or for an activity that directly relates to an income-producing asset, then you are allowed to claim the interest on any loan you have acquired to make the purchase or pay the expense.

The actual collateral you give to your lender to secure the loan (usually a property) does not determine the tax deductibility of the loan. So, you must note the following points:

- If you use your personal home as security for a loan to buy an investment property, the interest on the debt is tax-deductible, as the *purpose* for the loan is 'investment'.

- If you use your investment property as security for a loan to buy a personal home to live in, or any other personal-use asset or expense, the interest on the debt is *not* tax-deductible as the *purpose* for the debt is 'personal'.

- If you use an investment property and your personal home as security to borrow funds, only the interest on that portion of the funds directly relating to the investment (be it the one securing the loan or any other property you buy as an investment) can be claimed as a tax deduction.

- If you use an investment property as security to borrow funds to buy another investment property, and you tacked on a little extra for any items of a personal nature (such as a new kitchen in your own home or a holiday or car), you can only claim the interest accruing on the portion of the debt that was for investment purposes.

Note that you can have any loan structure you want, secured by whatever the bank will accept and you are not breaking the law. It is when you try to make a claim for interest or other expenses not of an investment nature that you are considered to be breaking the law. If you are aware of the 'purpose' test, it is very easy for you to work out for yourself what can legally be claimed and what cannot.

Lender's mortgage insurance

When we at Destiny® assist people to invest in property, usually we advise that they do not borrow any more than 80 per cent of the security they can offer. This is because if you borrow 80 per cent, you still own 20 per cent and if you are forced for some reason to sell up at a time when property values are stagnating, you can at least be sure of paying out your debts and costs and still having a little left over. Some people like to borrow with an even smaller loan to valuation ratio (the amount of loan as it relates to the value of your property), such as 70 per cent or lower, as this makes them feel even safer.

Others, however, like to take bigger risks and so wish to obtain mortgages as high as the bank will allow. Most banks will allow you to borrow up to 95 per cent of an owner-occupied home and up to 90 per cent of the value of an investment property.

Once you borrow more than 80 per cent, the bank seeks protection too. At 80 per cent, it is most likely that, in the event of a forced sale, the bank should at least recover what is outstanding, and enough to pay its costs of selling your property. At 90 per cent and 95 per cent, however, this may not be the case and a forced sale, particularly in the early years, may leave it short of the outstanding loan.

Because of this, the bank will require you to take out an insurance policy to protect it, and you will be the one who has to pay the premium on this. The premium on LMI rises on a pro rata basis depending on how high your loan to valuation ratio goes. So, while an 81 per cent LVR may result in an insurance premium of 0.1 per cent of the total loan amount, the premium on a 95 per cent LVR can be as high as 1.5 per cent of the loan amount. In addition, higher loan amounts will also attract higher premiums.

The premium is paid once only and is usually non-refundable, although if you refinance early in the loan it is worth asking about this, as a few mortgage insurers do offer a refund of some of the premium if refinanced in the first year. Further, if you have purchased a property that you believe has increased a great deal in the first year, it may be worth paying for another valuation, because if a new valuation proves that the existing loan is now below the 80 per cent mark, you may qualify for some premium rebate.

Home mortgage insurance

In the 1980s, most banks sold home mortgage insurance policies with the premiums being tacked onto your mortgage repayments. This insurance was designed to give you cover in the event of your untimely death—basically, the policy allowed for the balance of your mortgage to be repaid if you died. Many banks made it a condition of your loan that you took out this policy and they benefited by obtaining commissions on the product sale.

The Consumer Credit Code of 1996 made it illegal for lenders to make home mortgage insurance a requirement of credit and, for a time, these policies went out of favour.

Now it seems non-bank lenders are again offering them, optionally, again including the policy premiums in the loan repayments. It comes under many names such as mortgage protection insurance and loan protection insurance, to name a few, but the basic features are all the same.

If you are offered a policy of this nature, please ensure that you explore fully its features and benefits. Usually, with a policy such as this, the premium remains the same for the term of the loan while the payout decreases as your loan balance decreases. Often, a straight term life insurance policy, purchased independently of the loan from an insurance broker will offer better benefits for the same premium, without the payout figure decreasing.

Credit cards

If you are using a rapid mortgage reduction system, it is likely that you will have been advised to obtain a credit card with an interest-free period. The purpose for this is so that you can place any income you do earn in offset against your loan balance (thereby saving a small amount of interest) while you use the credit card to pay all of your expenses. When the credit card's payment falls due, all of it must be paid by drawing back out of your loan the money sitting in offset.

Be very careful if this is what you are planning. This can only work if you ensure that you always pay off your card, in full, when it falls due and if you stick to a budget and use your credit card only for legitimate expenses. Using a rapid mortgage reduction system per se will *not* result in your loan being paid off any earlier if you simply draw back out all of your funds (or more) each month. The amount of interest offset you gain, although it does snowball, will not result in a rapid decline of your loan balance if you continue to spend or overspend. It is the combined effect of committing your positive cash flow and as much extra funds of your own *as well as* using a credit card to delay bill paying that will enable you to pay off debt much sooner. We have found that, without exception, those of our clients who diligently use the Destiny® System of financial and loan management provided to them by us (a system of money management and property investing) always pay off their loans more quickly, while those who do not use the system and who do not pay attention to their budgets generally fail. Be sure you are aware that your credit card is not there to provide a means for you to buy those things you want sooner — it is simply an expense tool for you to pay the expenses you have planned for.

In addition, all credit cards are not the same. While the actual interest rate will not be important to you if you are using it well (that is, *never* incurring interest since you pay it off in full every month), the benefits may be. My husband and I use a card that gives us one frequent flyer point for each dollar spent, and, since we use the card for everything (personal, investment and business), <u>we get a lot of free travel!</u> Note, however, that these benefits are only useful to you if the card gives you the right kind of flexibility.

Summary

- Principal and interest loans should be used if you are not good at managing money.

- Interest-only loans are inflexible and do not allow you to pay off principal as quickly as you may wish.

- A line of credit can enable you to pay principal and interest or just interest, whichever is appropriate for you at the time.

- A well-used line of credit can result in less interest and a shorter term even if the interest rate is slightly higher, as long as you adopt a committed rapid mortgage reduction strategy.

- A line of credit has the flexibility, which means that one loan may last you a lifetime.

- Not all lines of credit are the same, so do your research well and seek guidance from experts.

- Your bank manager or loan broker may not be able to give you the best loan structure advice.

- Cross-collateralisation does not have any drawbacks and can give you some great advantages.

- Be very careful of any schemes advising you to capitalise investment debt—a claim on capitalised interest may not be legal.

- You can legally adopt a mortgage reduction strategy for your investment debt, but you must do this correctly.

- It is always the purpose of the loan that determines the tax deductibility of its interest, not the security given for the loan.

- Lender's mortgage insurance protects the lender where you have a loan with a high LVR.

- While home mortgage insurance protects your family or dependants in the event of your death, as it pays out the balance of your mortgage, it may not be the best sort of insurance.

- Credit cards should be used wisely and chosen for the added benefits they can give you.

Conclusion

So many people take such care when choosing property as an investment and planning their investment strategy. Yet often, those same people neglect their borrowing strategy and take advice from the wrong people, setting up structures and loans that cost them money and benefits and often the ability to leverage at a greater rate.

This aspect of your investing life requires great care and attention and a different approach to that you would take for a loan for a home of your own. Be very sure that you get help from professionals who really do know what they are talking about.

Chapter 6

To trust or not to trust
— structures and strategies

The rumour mill

Last year, I listened with great interest as a woman of some notoriety in the field of investment property seminars gave a presentation at one of the state money shows. In addition to her somewhat unsound advice to invest in Outer Mongolia or some other far-flung place, she told a story about a hapless golf enthusiast on Hamilton Island. In a momentary lapse of consciousness, he allegedly hit his ball straight into the head of the golfer in front of him, downing the poor fellow and killing him instantly. The family of the deceased sued, of course, and the ill-fated golfer lost all he owned.

The speaker claimed that had the golfer protected his assets by having them all in a family trust, the deceased's family would not have been able to seize them and the assets would have remained safe.

On the basis of this story, the advice was for everyone to race out and transfer all of their assets into a trust for protection. We are an increasingly litigious society, was the claim.

Had it been stated that there has been a noted increase in the number of people being stripped of their assets as a result of these kinds of lawsuits, or had statistics been displayed that showed a rapid increase of lawsuits in Australia over the past years, then I may have reason to agree that there is a case for setting up a structure that at best provides limited protection and at worst removes valuable tax breaks. But in truth, I believe that you have about as much chance of being sued, plausibly *or* frivolously, as you have of being kicked in the head by a donkey! To prove this, for the past two years, I have asked every audience I have addressed if any of them have ever been sued for anything other than possibly dubious business dealings, and I have not yet found one person who has.

Before you head off to your lawyer or accountant to set up what could possibly be a useless, costly structure of any kind, you must first become familiar with what is being offered and what it can do for you, if anything at all.

Discretionary family trusts

At every seminar I have conducted, there have been people who have asked if I think they should be setting up a trust structure for their investment strategy.

A discretionary family trust is a legal structure that is set up to hold assets or to receive income. Any income made from the assets and/or received into the trust must be distributed to the beneficiaries each year—income cannot be held over. Once the beneficiary has received the distribution, it is taxed at that person's marginal rate, and if this income results in the beneficiary falling into a higher rate of tax, then the higher rate applies. The term 'discretionary' refers to the fact that the trustees have the discretion to decide how much income, if any, is paid to each beneficiary.

Beneficiaries up to the age of 18 years will attract 'children's tax' (on unearned income) of up to 66 per cent once their total income, including beneficiary income, reaches the limit as defined by the tax office for that year (at the time of writing, this is around $500). Once children reach 18, they are regarded as adults and pay tax at normal individual rates.

In past years, these types of structures were often used by self-employed tradespeople as a way of income-splitting. They would divert all earned income into the trust and split it with a spouse, who may have been employed part-time or considered a partner of the business. Small amounts could also be distributed tax-free to children. In more recent times, the tightening of rules has meant that the income from businesses such as these must be split according to personal exertion — in order for a spouse to receive distributions from business income passed through a trust, there must be evidence that he or she is contributing labour, or effort and influence, commensurate with the distribution. This has led to the disuse of many trusts.

Today, people are being advised to set up a trust structure for the purchase of investment property. Trusts can borrow to invest and the trust then owns the asset. The stated benefits for using a trust to buy investment property include:

- the ability to distribute the income to beneficiaries who are in low tax brackets

- the ability to protect assets in the event that you are sued

- the ability to avoid tax in the future once the property becomes positively geared (that is, when debt is paid down and rents rise).

Conversely, I believe there are many reasons you should decide not to use a trust structure. These are as follows.

- Ask around your circle of friends and determine how many people you know who have been sued. As I mentioned previously, I have never met anyone who has been frivolously sued (sued for outrageous reasons) and I also don't know anyone who has been plausibly sued. I am often told by readers that they are worried that a tenant may sue them, but I remind them that public liability insurance (which is included in all landlord's insurance policies), usually prescribes $10 million of cover and the e days there is a cap on claims for anyone injuring the selves that is well below this amount. So, as long as you are not involved in any unscrupulous business activit r are not in the medical profession or another hig profession, then it is most unlikely your assets need rotecting to that extent.

- Even if you are sued and your assets are in a trust, this does not mean they are necessarily protected. Both the Australian Securities & Investments Commission (ASIC) and, in the case of divorce, the Family Court have the power to unwind a trust to reach assets in the event that creditors, litigants or spouses need to be paid. If ASIC believes you have set up a trust in 'contemplation of being sued' then it can seize trust-protected assets. So, if you are involved in dodgy business dealings, or you are otherwise trying to 'hide' your assets for any reason, a trust probably won't protect you anyway.

- A trust pays no tax. Positive cash flow from property is a result of making tax claims, the benefits of which make up the margin in your cash flow and give you extra money each week. The higher the tax bracket you are in, the more tax you get back from your claims and the greater the likelihood of seeing a positive cash flow from your investments. If you buy your property in a trust, then the entity that owns the asset (the trust) cannot enjoy the tax benefits (as it pays no tax), and the entity that receives the income (the beneficiaries) has no access to tax benefits to offset the extra income received. At first, there may be little income (especially if expenses exceed income) but in later years, as debt decreases and rents rise, there will be income. This income must be distributed every year and will be tacked onto the top of any other income earned, possibly taking the recipient into a higher tax bracket.

- While it is true that once retired, you may be in a very low tax bracket and the trust can then distribute as it sees fit to those who pay the lowest tax, the facts are that most trusts are set up with only one or two parties to the property transaction as beneficiaries — usually spouses or partners. By the time you do retire, you may well have many properties earning a lot of income that must be distributed each year anyway. Having the income flow through the trust will do very little, if anything, to change the amount of tax you ultimately pay when it ends up in your hands. The only way this would be any different would be if you also had other people, such as your children, as beneficiaries. This means you are either giving them an income (why would you do that? You are the one who is retired and who needs it!), or distributing it to them so they can give it back to you. If you are doing this, they are probably already earning other income by then, and so tax at high rates will still be levied on the income. If they are still under 18, then they pay 66 per cent on any tax above the very small tax-free threshold.

The realities are that if you build a substantial portfolio, you are going to pay a lot of tax regardless of whether you receive the income in the hand or whether it flows through a trust first. I simply cannot see any real benefit in buying property in a trust. It *fails* as an asset-protection tool, it *fails* as a tax shelter, and, as I said before, all it does is remove those tax benefits that are so important in the early years in helping you to build a bigger portfolio (as they give you important cash flow *today* when you need it most).

Actually, come to think of it, I *can* see a benefit—to the person you pay to set it up, and to the person you pay to audit and prepare the tax returns on it!

Hybrid discretionary trusts

The older I become, the more I see new tax loopholes being found and exploited—that is, exploited until the tax office gets on to them and closes them up again. I have yet to see a scheme that aims to get around taxation that has not been closed off pretty quickly. No doubt, the advent of the hybrid discretionary trust is another such arrangement, just waiting to be targeted.

This type of trust is a combination trust. It uses a family trust, as outlined earlier, in combination with a unit trust. A unit trust is another type of legal structure where a trust is formed (with trustees who have legal responsibility for the assets) and divided up into individual units, each of which has a price. People then purchase the units, and are able to borrow money to fund the purchase. The funds the trust raises are then invested into the family trust, which uses these funds to buy property. Because the units are an income-producing investment, <u>the investor can claim the interest on the loan used to buy them as a tax deduction.</u> All income then flows through the family trust to be distributed in the manner most tax-effective to the beneficiaries.

and the trust is not fixed

Any website or article that mentions these types of trusts cautions investors to be very careful of who they seek advice from when setting up these structures, as few people know how they really work. I suspect this is because they are, in fact, a tax loophole and, so far, I have not found anything in any legislation to support the hybrid trust theory. Let us assume for a minute that there *is* a loophole that can be accessed by setting up this complex structure — always remember that if you take advantage of these untested arrangements, you may be exposing yourself to harsh penalties under the general anti-avoidance provisions of the tax legislation (Part IVA).

And besides, who really wants to make investing that difficult? As I have said many times before, 10 to 15 years of hard, smart work and you will set up an income for life anyway. Be honest and no-one will sue you, and purchase landlord's insurance so that if a tenant does, you have a policy to protect you. You will make much more money than you need and you will not have to spend unnecessary money on audits and administration, or have a Harvard degree to understand what you are doing!

In good company?

Another favourite tactic of accountants looking for an extra dollar (please excuse my cynicism) is to advise their clients to set up a company in which to buy property. The theory here is that the company holds the assets (the property) and only pays 30 per cent tax on the income.

Again, this theory ignores the fact that if you intend to buy positive cash flow property, the cash flow is probably negative until you receive the tax breaks. By using a company structure, you are intentionally setting your potential tax breaks at a maximum of 30 per cent, when it may be possible that if you purchase property as an individual, you may be in a higher bracket than that.

The other thing that people do not realise is that company tax only applies while funds stay in the company. The minute that you make drawings from the company and the funds hit your hand, they are tacked on top of other income you may have earned and you pay tax at whatever marginal rate of tax you then attract. If the funds have already paid tax at 30 per cent, you must still pay the difference. So, as the properties begin to make real money (due to a lessening of debt and an increase in rents), you will want to have the cash and you have no choice but to draw it down and pay whatever tax is due on it.

Lastly, not only do companies lose the concession on capital gains tax (individuals receive a 50 per cent discount on capital gains tax), but, in reality, a company is meant to be set up to run a business. The tax office expects that at some time in the future the company will make a profit. You are not supposed to be setting up a company just to buy property unless you plan for it to be a property investment company. Once you do this, many things change and your requirements to operate as a business as well as the higher costs of running a company compliantly may make the whole strategy far too complicated.

In whose name?

We have now discovered that many of the complex structures being proposed today offer very little in the way of true benefits and much in the way of confusion and complications. It is clear that the best way to buy property is in the name of the individual—the greatest tax breaks are possible this way and with the assistance of the tax breaks you can build a larger portfolio, more quickly.

It is important to know, then, in whose name you should buy the property. If you are a single person, that is easy—you buy it in your name! But if you are buying with someone else, perhaps a spouse, friend or relative, then it may not be quite this clear-cut. The structure you choose depends on a number of things, which are discussed below.

Joint names/joint tenants

Where the two (or more) parties earn similar incomes, and this is expected to continue indefinitely, then you should purchase income-producing assets in joint names and as joint tenants. When you do this, you share income, expenses and tax benefits equally.

In addition to this, the joint tenancy arrangement means that where one party dies, the assets fall 'outside of the estate' and are automatically transferred to the surviving tenant(s).

Joint names/tenants in common

When you purchase property in joint names and as tenants in common, you can elect to share income and expenses in any way you wish, and the proportions you choose must be noted on the title.

For example, you may wish to share the income and expenses on an 80/20 basis and this is what the title will reflect. Forevermore, income and expenses must be shared according to this original formula, so you must be very sure that the benefits of the split arrangement you choose are lasting, and that circumstances in the future will not make the arrangement less favourable.

In addition to the ability to elect the sharing proportions, each owner in a tenants in common arrangement has the right to will his or her share to anyone he or she chooses — that share falls inside his or her estate and upon death becomes willable.

Partnership arrangements

Clients of mine have advised that their accountants suggested they set up a partnership agreement, which then allows them to buy property as joint tenants but share the income and expenses in any way they see fit. The terms of this agreement overrule the tenancy arrangements and doing this can mean that the choice of how the income and expenses are split can change each year, depending on where it is needed most. So, for example, in the first year it may be decided that both parties need an equal amount of tax benefits and so the partnership agreement allocates income and expenses equally. The following year, one party may have earned more income elsewhere, and so the decision is made in that year to allot more of the income and expenses, and so tax benefits, to that party.

While it is possible to operate under a partnership agreement for tax purposes when investing in property, the tax office does state that to do so, you must be carrying on the 'business of rental properties'. While there is no specific number of properties you need to own to be considered to be carrying on the business of rental properties, the tax office stipulates that a combination of the number of properties and the time and effort involved in conducting the business can clearly determine if a business is in operation.

For example, if a couple owned 20 properties that were managed by a managing agent, and repaired and maintained by tradespeople, they would not be considered to be operating a rental property business. Tax treatment of this couple would be as individuals, and no partnership agreement can change the original intent of the tenancy arrangements. However, if that couple owned 20 properties that they managed, repaired, supervised and perhaps even traded from time to time, then clearly they are operating a business, and for tax purposes they may be treated according to any partnership agreement they had drawn up.

I caution against thinking that setting up a partnership may be a nice tax dodge—you really have to be involved in the bulk of the work and supervision of your property to prove you are in the business, and you may well lose tax advantages, such as discounted capital gains tax, and other benefits once you turn this process into a business in this way.

Choosing an enduring structure

Recently, I set up a loan for a good friend who was buying property. After I received a copy of the purchase contracts, I called him in alarm to find out why he was putting the property in his name. He told me it was because he had read one of my books and it clearly stated that property should be purchased in the name of the highest income earner. Since he earned $80 000 per annum and his wife earned $25 000, the property needed to go in his name.

He was only half-right! When you are buying property with another party(s), there are two very important tasks you must perform before deciding in whose name you will buy. These are:

1. You must establish how the cash flow is being made. If it is positive cash flow, then this means that the cash flow is being made mostly as a result of the tax break. Most probably, the expenses on the property *exceed* the income and the difference is made up by the tax breaks that come from the on-paper deductions. If this is the case, then you will want the property to be purchased in the name of the person who pays the most tax, so that you can get the most tax back.

    If, however, the property makes its cash flow by being positively geared (that is, the income *exceeds* the expenses), then you will want to put the property in the name of the person who earns the least income. This is due to the fact that when a property earns a raw cash flow because it makes more in rent than you spend on it, you must pay tax on the gain. You will want a property such as this to be held in the name of the person who pays the least tax.

2. You must determine if the situation regarding your tax position is expected to remain the same for the long term.

If you know of any reason why, at some time in the near future, the situation may change, then you must calculate the costs and benefits and work out whose name to buy it in for the greatest benefit over the long term. The following example illustrates this point.

Do something similar to this!

Tony and Janet earn $80 000 and $20 000 respectively. They are looking at buying a positive cash flow property and plan on buying it in Tony's name as he gets a higher tax return.

Janet, however, plans to return to her full-time IT job in three years' time. At that time, she will be earning $130 000 per year.

Looking at the next 10 years, let's imagine that the property they are considering has on-paper losses of $5000 per annum. Tony and Janet's options are as follows.

- If they buy the property in Tony's name only, he will receive $1500 tax back per year, for a total tax return over 10 years of $15 000.

- If they buy the property in joint names, in the first three years they will receive a yearly tax break of $750 for Tony and $425 for Janet ($1175 per year, less than what Tony alone could get). In the next seven years, they will receive $750 a year for Tony and $1175 for Janet ($1925 per year). The total tax break would be $17 000.

- If they buy the property in Janet's name only, in the first three years they will receive a tax break of just $850 per year (considerably less than what Tony alone would receive), and then $2350 a year for the next seven years. The total tax break would be $19 000.

From this illustration, you can see that it is considerably better for Tony and Janet to accept a smaller tax return for the next three years so that they can obtain a greater return in the following years.

Before making any decision about whose name to buy a property in, not only must you ascertain the party most likely to get the greatest tax benefits, you must also determine if the situation is expected to remain the same in the years to come. Whatever strategy you choose, great care and attention needs to be paid to the initial structure and its ability to continue to provide the greatest benefits in future years, and you should always choose to seek expert advice.

Guarantors

While the subject of becoming a guarantor for another person is essentially information that belongs in chapter 5, when investing in property the issue of being a guarantor is most likely to arise when choosing the method of ownership.

Most commonly, when two parties make the decision to buy property they will be married to each other or life partners and the 'deposit' they use to purchase the property will be in the form of equity in a property they already own together. Since an owner-occupied home does not attract any tax concessions, the choice of ownership structure for the personal residence is generally an easy one, with most parties choosing to be joint tenants.

As the family home will probably be used as collateral security alongside the new investment property, and the two (or more) securities will most likely be cross-collateralised (covered earlier in chapter 5), then, where it has been decided that the ownership of the new property should be given to only one of the parties, it is likely the bank will require the other person (the one who is an owner on the family home but not a legal owner on the investment property) to become a guarantor on the investment purchase loan. Note that this only occurs where both properties are being tied together in the one loan, as is most often the case where the equity from the first property is being used to help secure the purchase of the second property.

Typically, and if a line of credit with the ability to split is being used, the loan will have two accounts—one designated to represent any debt on the family home and one representing the debt on the new property. The first account will be in the names of the joint titleholders of the family home. The second account will be in the name of the titleholder of the new investment. The bank wants to make sure that the second party, whose name *does not* appear on the second account, understands that in the event that the party whose name *is* on the account stops repaying the loan or in any other way defaults, he or she is responsible for the full debt. As such, the bank will ask this party to be a guarantor.

Do not let this situation worry you in any way. Being a guarantor carries pretty much the same obligations as being a borrower, so there are no additional requirements or awful things that can happen to you by agreeing to be a guarantor.

If you are worried that your spouse/partner may indeed default and leave you holding the entire debt yourself, then perhaps you should not be investing with them in the first place!

Buying with others

Opportunities may arise where you are invited to invest in property with someone who is *not* your spouse or life partner. Where you have limited funds or equity of your own, this may seem like a chance to gain a foothold in the property investment market.

If you are considering this as an option, there are several issues to consider before proceeding. These include the following:

- This arrangement will essentially be a partnership in its physical sense and so you must be prepared for the fact that partnerships often do not work out. In the future, many issues may arise that you will not agree on and this can result in a loss of friendship or a falling out with family members.

- If borrowing is involved (as it most likely will be), the situation may become complicated. As we are jointly and severally responsible for any loan we take out with another party, the entire amount of the loan will be considered to be each party's responsibility. This means that, should you in the future wish to borrow more money, perhaps for an investment you undertake alone, the commitment to the *entire loan* will be regarded as yours, and this may reduce your potential to borrow additional funds.

- Where the property you buy with someone else increases in value, you will only be able to leverage against that equity if you buy more property with that party. The equity will not be available to you personally to use elsewhere.

- Rapid mortgage reduction is very difficult to undertake with a party who is not your spouse. You cannot both place all of your income and rents into the loan and then draw out your respective expenses as they are likely to be unequal.

- If the other party experiences financial difficulty, at best you will be left paying the debt alone. At worst, the asset you own half of may be seized to satisfy any unrelated, outstanding debts of your fellow investor.

- If your needs change or the needs of your fellow investor changes, owning property with him or her can be a difficult arrangement to quickly unwind.

Be very sure you understand the full implications of investing with someone you do not otherwise share your life with and consider all of the possible outcomes (positive *and* negative) before proceeding.

Testamentary trust

Often, after I have given people my take on the need (or lack of) to set up a trust or company in which to place their investments, they bring up one last worry—that should they die, their children will inherit their properties and consequently be up for all sorts of taxes, charges and problems.

There is a way you can provide for your assets to be effectively distributed to your beneficiaries without going through the costly, and often disadvantageous, process of setting up a family trust, and that is to ensure you put in place provisions for a testamentary trust to be created in the event of your death.

A testamentary trust is similar to a discretionary trust—once created there is a trustee(s) and beneficiary(s), and you choose who these will be by leaving instructions in your will.

There are some very important differences between a testamentary and a family trust that make them excellent asset and income-protection tools.

There is no trust deed, as the trust is automatically created when you die, based on the wishes expressed in your will. In addition, there is no restriction on distributions to children as in a family trust, where, as mentioned earlier, any distributions over and above the low threshold of around $500 are taxed at 66 per cent.

Instead, distributions to children are taxed at normal adult rates, which means the first $6000 (at the time of writing) is tax-free, and any distributions over and above this are taxed at the normal marginal rates of tax.

Take a look at the following example.

Edith and Joe are 79 years of age. They have three children, all in their late-40s, who each have two children in their teens. Edith and Joe own $200 000 worth of managed funds and three investment properties.

If they pass on and leave all of these assets to their children, the children will have immediate tax issues as they all already earn good incomes.

Instead, Edith and Joe draw up a will with a testamentary trust being created to leave their assets to their children and then the grandchildren.

This means that Edith and Joe's children then control the assets and have the ability to channel the income to their own children. The assets are held in the name of the trust, with the trustees (the children) having complete discretion over where the income is distributed. Instead of the children receiving the income, and losing almost half of it in tax, they could pay each grandchild $6000 a year, tax-free.

The grandchildren can do what they like with the money, or their parents can elect that they spend it on items that they would otherwise have to pay for, such as school fees and uniforms. Essentially, the parents now benefit from this distribution without the tax hassles. Once Edith and Joe's children stop working, they can then begin to take distributions, with all of the tax benefits for pensioners applying.

Since the assets are held by the trust, not by the children directly, they are protected from creditors in the event that any of the children experience financial difficulty. When these children pass on, the trust has already determined that the assets pass to the grandchildren. This means that there will be no costs to transfer the assets to them as the assets are not transferred at all—they remain the property of the trust. The trust can go in on perpetuity for many generations to come.

Whatever arrangements you choose to make regarding your ownership structure, you must seek out the help of a professional. Each circumstance will be different and the information in this book may not apply to you at all. Only a qualified person can tell you what is really right for you.

Summary

- Setting up a family trust to hold your investment properties has no great benefits. It reduces your tax benefits and cannot provide guaranteed asset protection.

- Since a family trust must distribute its income every year, even when you retire you will still be required to receive the income and pay tax on it. Channelling the income through the trust will not provide any real benefit unless you plan to give away most of the income to other beneficiaries.

- A company structure is not appropriate for anyone wishing to buy positive cash flow property, as tax is paid at lower rates.

- Once income is taken from a company into an individual's hands, normal tax rates will apply.

- Opting for a company structure will mean you lose concessional capital gains tax benefits.

- Buying property as joint tenants means that you share all income and expenses. Each party's share falls automatically to the other party on death.

- Buying property as tenants in common allows you to split income and expenses unequally. Upon death, each party may will their share to whomever they wish.

- A partnership arrangement generally will not overrule the legal ownership structure for tax purposes.

- You should consider the long-term tax position before deciding in whose name to buy.

- Where two parties want to share one loan for a property where only one party's name appears on the title, the other party may be required by the bank to become a guarantor.

- Take great care if you are buying property with someone who does not otherwise share your life.

- If you wish for your assets to be more effective for your beneficiaries upon your death, you can create a testamentary trust in your will that will provide many benefits to those to whom you are bequeathing your assets.

Conclusion

Life is not meant to be easy, but property investing is! Apart from those in the medical profession who may genuinely be exposed to some risk of litigation that their professional indemnity insurance cannot cover, I have yet to meet any person who has a real need to set up the types of complicated structures I have outlined in this chapter. Once you do so it adds a whole realm of administrative requirements, supervision and cost without a commensurate amount of real benefits.

Remember the KISS principle when you invest — 'keep it straight and simple' — and you will not only enjoy your investing a lot more, you will achieve a great deal more, too.

Chapter 7 _____

Scams, spruikers and secrets

_____

Sex, lies and videotape

You know, just starting to write this chapter, I can feel my
blood pressure rising and a real tension creep into my spine.
While I am deciding what I will write about, I am thinking of
the countless number of people—good, honest and trusting
people—who have approached me at a seminar or expo with
a story of sincere woe about a greedy opportunist taking their
money from them. It's easy to suggest that people should not
be so gullible, but often the players in these dishonest games
are veterans of conning others and devising ruthless schemes to
line their own pockets. They are masters of taking advantage of
people's genuine desire to safeguard their financial futures.

In writing this chapter, I want to make you aware of just a small
handful of the sorts of schemes you chould look out for. I will
only scratch the surface, however, and you should be wary of
everyone and anyone who seems to be offering you a way to cut

corners and join the wealthy people of tomorrow by following their simple rules for success.

Success is not simple. Ask anyone referred to as an 'overnight success' and he or she will tell you that the 'night' was 20 years or so long! Conversely, talk to these supposed experts about the strategies they are teaching you and ask them how much money they have personally made out of them — I can almost guarantee you that it has been none! Look instead to how they really make their money and you will almost certainly discover that it has been from the unscrupulous manner in which they have delivered their lies and deceit to the unsuspecting public, charging thousands of dollars for information that has little chance of even working in the real world.

Let's take a look at some of the more common scams, strategies and spruiking methods you may find in Australia today.

The seminar

I conduct seminars all over Australia every year, hoping to provide people with education. I make my living doing what I teach others to do (that is, investing in positive cash flow property) and from providing personal financial advising services through my Destiny® branches. That being the case, I believe that education should be as free as I can make it, so I charge a small fee usually around $25, to pay for the venue and equipment hire costs.

At that seminar, people are surprised to find that I don't have a big weekend event (or 'boot camp', as some spruikers are calling it) on offer for the lucky few who can come up with the many thousands of dollars required to attend. What they get on the night is all they get, and they can add much more to their knowledge base through my books. Other people don't come at all because they have a notion that, at $25, the information couldn't be that useful.

How sad it is that the country has now come to this — a society that expects that the more you pay for your education, the better it must be. Based on this fact, I see many people who lack any kind of qualification or any real-life experience, staging seminars at incredible costs that do little more than instantly line their own pockets with wealth. And, it seems, the more they charge, the more people are willing to flock to them. Some even use credit to pay for the courses in the hope that some secret will be revealed that will make it all work like magic.

While there are many varieties of the 'get rich quick' seminar, in most cases you will be exposed to these schemes in the following way:

1. You will be 'telemarketed' by someone who asks you about your home loan or if you are interested in wealth creation.

2. You will be invited to attend a 'free seminar'. Sometimes the deal is sweetened by the offer of something else — a free weekend holiday if you come along, a free book or some other bribe.

3. When you attend, the basis of the seminar will be information designed to make you worry about your future — statistics (often without a source quoted) about poverty, income levels or expected pension rates. You will be offered a 'glimpse' of a potential opportunity for you to be the one who avoids this coming catastrophe if you are lucky.

4. The opportunity will be one of two things — either the purchase of property being sold by the company represented by the seminar presenter, or the chance to attend another seminar, at a special discounted price for those people who sign up on the night. Sometimes you may be offered both.

5. Other variations on this theme exist—the chance to purchase 'wealth packages' for thousands of dollars, using credit or payment plans, the chance to be a part of a small, select group of people who are given special information that no-one else ever has the privilege to hear, an opportunity to be one of only six people to receive a special discount on a property, or a special bonus like a boat or a holiday, if you sign up that evening.

These seminars have common features, including:

*   Upbeat music—such as the theme from the *Rocky* films, *Star Wars* music and/or the kind of melodies that tend to make your blood pump faster and create an atmosphere of excitement.

*   Adoring disciples—seemingly ordinary people, often former 'students', who swear that they were once just like you but that this presenter changed their lives and they are now earning many hundreds of thousands of dollars a year.

*   The promise of 'secrets' being revealed or of fabulous wealth.

*   Blatant signs of the 'success' of the presenter—pictures of him or her sitting on a Ferrari, for example.

*   The use of company names designed to instill comfort in you—words like 'institute', 'academy' 'success' or names that create an aura of corporate conservatism—for example, 'Bentley, Bush and Associates'.

*   Presenters who seem to say a lot but who actually say very little—one victim reports that when he mentioned he was confused, he was told, 'Confusion is good because it means you are opening up to new ideas,' whatever that is supposed to mean!

- Expressions used by presenters—'Money for jam!', 'No money down!', 'Double your money in two months!', 'Stunning results!', 'Incredible riches!', 'Secrets you will never be told anywhere else!' and the like.

- Some type of special offer that must be taken up on the day—there are thousands of examples, such as discounts off the 'boot camp' or a special investor bonus of additional, super-secret information for early-bird registrations.

Be extremely careful about attending these types of seminars. They will make you feel motivated. You will be buoyed by the apparent success of others and by the atmosphere they have tried to create to seduce you. You will find it incredibly difficult to say no, and the people employed to help you say yes will do everything in their power to get you into some kind of 'contract' on the day that may be very difficult to get out of.

I can honestly say that I have rarely seen a seminar in this vein that has actually been anything other than a con. Make sure that, before you attend, you know exactly what is going to happen. Here are some questions you can ask before signing up to attend that will go some way toward protecting yourself:

- Who is the presenter and what are his or her qualifications?

- What kinds of licences/tertiary qualifications does the company or its directors have?

- Has there ever been any type of action—legal or otherwise—taken against the company?

- Has ASIC asked any kind of questions about the company or the presenter at any time in the past, or carried out an investigation or issued any kind of warning? Be sure to visit the ASIC website at www.asic.gov.au to run a free 'safety check' on the company.

- Has the company or presenter been the subject of any investigation by any state Office of Fair Trading, Consumer Affairs department, or the Australian Consumer and Competition Commission (ACCC)? Check the websites of the Office of Fair Trading in your state and the ACCC for more information.

- Can the presenter demonstrate that he or she has successfully applied the principles being taught him- or herself?

- Has the presenter or company received any serious complaint from previous attendees of any seminar or workshop they have conducted?

- Will attendees be invited to take part in any other seminar or workshop, or be asked to sign up to any fee-for-service program while attending the seminar?

- Does the seminar aim to sell any asset, such as property, shares or managed funds, to the attendees at any time during or after the seminar?

While this list of questions is not exhaustive and will still not protect you against determined scammers, it may go some way toward helping you to sort out whether a seminar is genuinely educational or a money-making venture for the presenter and his or her company.

Wraps

There are currently a number of players in the wrapping game who tell stories of personal riches obtained using this method of property investing. I am not convinced that any of these people have actually created wealth from this strategy or from any of the other questionable strategies they also spruik. What I do know is that all of them claim that wrapping is the next greatest thing in wealth creation, yet none of them are prepared to outline the considerable disadvantages of this approach.

In a nutshell, wraps work like this:

The investor (hereto known as the 'wrapper') purchases a property for, say, $200 000. The wrapper applies for a loan from the bank and pays, say, 7 per cent interest on that loan.

The wrapper then approaches a potential homebuyer who is currently renting and who wants to own a home of their own, but for some reason cannot borrow—they may be credit-impaired or simply cannot afford the repayments and so do not satisfy bank lending criteria. The wrapper 'sells' the property to the homebuyer with a contract that settles at a pre-determined time in the future—say, three years—at a price greater than what the wrapper paid, but less than it should be worth when the time comes. In the meantime, the buyer lives in the house for a 'rental' payment, which is actually a loan repayment. However, since the wrapper is now taking on some risk (in selling to a person who cannot borrow), he or she not only adds a premium to the house price (and sells for, say, $220 000), he or she also adds a premium to the interest rate (say, 3 per cent).

The theory goes that in three years' time, when the contract is ready to settle, and with the benefit of the property 'doubling' every 10 years (increasing by 7 per cent per annum, so it is now worth $245 000), the tenant/purchaser will now be able to refinance the $220 000 at standard bank rates, as he or she now has some equity in the home. The wrapper, meanwhile, has made a cool $7000-per-year premium on the interest rate ($21 000), plus the initial $20 000 profit. Multiply this by, say, 10 wrap contracts at a time and the wrapper has made $410 000 cash for him- or herself in just three short years. Sounds perfect!

Here are the catches as I see them:

- The property remains in the wrapper's name up until the pre-agreed time to settle. The wrappee has no protection until the title is transferred.

- If the buyer cannot refinance at that time, the wrapper keeps the home and all repayments are forfeited.

- If the buyer defaults on repayments at any time throughout the contract, the wrapper keeps the home and all repayments are forfeited.

- If the property market falters even a tiny bit, then the buyer is disadvantaged.

- The premium paid on the interest rate usually makes the 'rent' repayments at least double that of standard rent returns. In these cases it would probably make much more financial sense for the buyer to simply wait and save up to buy his or her own house outright.

- The 'real' price of the home at the time of settlement is actually a lot more than the pre-agreed price, by the time you add on the premium paid on the interest rate. In the above example, the real price paid is almost the same as the 'expected' future value, so the purchaser could have just waited. If the market does not grow, the real price paid will be well over true market value.

While I have no empathy for wrappers who experience drawbacks (since, in my opinion, they are simply preying on the weak and less fortunate for their own material gains), it should be noted that there are dangers to the wrappers. These include:

- If the buyer defaults, he or she may in turn default on his or her own bank loan. I would consider this high risk given the dubious financial backgrounds of the people who usually become wrappees.

- The agreed price may fall well short of actual market value if a property boom occurs during the term.

- The wrapper may be required to pay capital gains tax without being eligible for the concession, since in reality the contract date is the day on which the contract becomes unconditional and will usually be within 12 months of the wrapper making the original purchase.

Wrapping is immoral and fraught with danger. Stay away from these schemes and question the professional ethics and other teachings of anyone who recommends this as a strategy.

Renovators

I have seen people purchase property, apply their considerable knack for renovating (as well as a considerable amount of their time), and sell the same property a short time later for a substantial gain.

I have seen dozens, even hundreds, more people who had the same idea but could not pull it off, spending time and money to make no more time or money for themselves at the end of the process.

I watched a seminar once where the presenter suggested that you could buy a property, cut the lawns, tidy the gardens and move the front door and sell it three months later for $50 000 more. He even claimed to have done the very same himself.

Forgive my cynicism but if indeed the property had been purchased and sold three months later for $50 000 more, I suggest that this was more due to the fact that the property may have been acquired at well under the market rate, right at the time that property in that area was about to experience an unprecedented boom. The property was probably also sold to someone who wanted exactly that property. A lick of paint and a tidy does not add anywhere near that kind of value to property.

Last year, in my capacity as host of a radio real estate show, I interviewed a TV renovation team about a house they were renovating in my local area. Their claim was that they could spend $15 000 and attract a much higher price for a property at auction, and the implication was that, by watching the show, you could learn to have the same sort of results.

I asked many questions and discovered that the entire project involved not just the six people from the team who appeared in front of the cameras, but an entire truckload of 50 more team members, who actually performed the labour.

Now, assuming that the non-television team members were each paid $35 an hour (which is low considering they worked weekends and after hours), in total, the value of the labour alone for the 14 hours a day over two days was at least $49 000. Add to that the material costs of $15 000 and you now have a true renovation cost of $64 000. In the entire time I watched that show, I never saw one house actually gain anywhere near that amount in increased sale price.

And so I come to my point. By the time you take into account the material costs and the true cost of your time, and then deduct the capital gains tax you will pay on the gain (which is only discounted if you hold the property for 12 months or more), then the chances that you will make real profits from this kind of renovating and trading are very small. Even if you can make money this way, you have to be good at renovating (since once you outsource the job you will severely cut your profits), you need time on your hands and you must purchase property that is as close to you as you can get it (since travelling to and from a property some distance away is simply not feasible). For busy people who want to build a portfolio that will one day provide the income to allow them to leave the paid workforce, this is simply not an option.

Buying 'off-the-plan' to sell for profits

A perfect market with stable growth would indicate that you could buy a property 'off-the-plan' (that is, yet to be built) at today's value with a long-dated settlement and then, just before settlement becomes due, sell it to someone else for a profit. This way you don't even need to borrow any money as you will never take actual ownership of the property.

In real life, it very rarely seems to work this way and the danger for people trying this is great.

Firstly, developers do try to sell off-the-plan property for a price that is somewhere in between today's prices and the expected future price, given stable and consistent growth. This means that if those expected future values are not achieved, the buyer may well lose out. He or she will be required to proceed with the purchase (or lose the deposit) and he or she may then have to take out the loan after all to proceed with the purchase.

I recently heard about a retired couple with very little in the way of savings, who had signed two contracts to purchase two off-the-plan properties that were due to settle in three years. The contract price was $400 000 each and the couple was led to expect that at the time of settlement, these properties would be worth $500 000 each, netting them $200 000. They used a deposit bond to secure the contract, so essentially it was a 'no money down' strategy designed to boost their retirement savings. They never planned to settle on the properties, and the whole deal had been orchestrated by a 'friend' who was a financial adviser.

When the settlement date came, they placed the properties on the market. The highest offer they had was $375 000, which was not enough. Their problem was compounded by the fact that they did not qualify to borrow any money to proceed as they were already retired. Although they used no money to secure the contract, instead using a deposit bond, in the event that they defaulted on the purchase contract, the insurance company would pay their forfeited deposit of $80 000 and sue them to recover these monies. Their 'friend', the financial adviser was still set to receive his commission of $15 000 per property once the sale eventually went through, bearing no responsibility for the poor advice he had provided them.

Another drawback is that many off-the-plan contracts have a clause in them allowing the developer to pull out of the deal, at any time, for any reason. There have been many purchasers who have bought property off the plan and when, some years later and just before settlement it is actually worth more than they agreed, find that the developer exercises his or her rights to terminate and pulls out of the deal, preferring instead to reap the profits him- or herself. Developers who do this have used the buyers' promises to buy (which are expressed in their purchase contracts), to raise funds from lenders to proceed with their developments, only to keep the profits and provide no reward to the buyers.

It is incredibly sad to see people caught up in this kind of trap, and off-the-plan purchases are particularly dangerous as you are dealing with the unknown future. It is definitely not an appropriate strategy for someone to undertake if he or she is in a weak financial position to begin with.

Rent guarantees

Rent guarantees themselves are not necessarily bad things and, for some people, they can provide a comfort and security to someone wishing to buy a property that seems a good investment for many reasons.

However, as I go on to explain, you should never consider buying a property that has little else going for it besides the rent guarantee.

A rent guarantee is a promise to pay an agreed sum for a pre-agreed term. It is not a promise to secure a tenant, nor is it a guarantee that the property can attract the amount of rent specified in the agreement. The 'guarantor' has no legal obligation to prove that he or she can actually finance this promise, nor is he or she required to give any evidence as to how the amount of the guarantee was arrived at.

Geoff was a client of mine who got carried away with the promises of a clever, silver-tongued marketing agent. Geoff's parents had successfully scooped up a substantial chunk of Sydney's Northern Beaches market, and he was taken in by the glossy brochures advertising the latest 'hotel unit' in an attractive beachside holiday spot. The 10-year guarantee would allow him to throw cash into his debt and by the time the guarantee expired, he would be the outright owner. Geoff truly felt that the strategy simply could not lose!

Eight months into the rent guarantee, the hotel operator went into liquidation, as occupancy levels of just 21 per cent had drained it of cash reserves. Geoff was left without an income and with a large debt. He went from expecting a cash flow of $4000 per annum after costs to paying out $9000 just to support the loan. He couldn't rent the property because it was just a hotel room with no kitchen. He couldn't sell it because of its bad rental history. The rent guarantee had masked the potential true underlying return of this property and provided false security for the buyers—the economics simply didn't stack up.

Rent guarantees aren't worth the paper they are written on. They cannot magically heal the sickness of an investment that was never going to work. They cannot stem the slow loss of capital as the properties bleed internally through poor management. They cannot make tenants suddenly materialise and they cannot heighten the attractiveness of any property if the market simply does not demand the accommodation.

And if a property needs a rent guarantee in order to attract buyers—what is wrong with it? Without rental demand and a vibrant economy, all a rent guarantee can ever do is temporarily blind investors to the facts. As far as I am concerned, the only true guarantee that a 'rent guarantee' can give is one that you are probably being swindled!

Buying overseas

Buying overseas or, at least, in New Zealand, is currently emerging as the next best thing for property investors. Why on earth you would want to complicate your investing life that much when there is an abundance of perfectly acceptable opportunities right here in our very own country is beyond me! I think that, often, the desire to invest overseas has more to do with isolated, sometimes relatively insignificant, facts that people discover—for example, the fact that New Zealand has no stamp duties or capital gains tax may seem attractive, but in the big picture it may not make the drawbacks worthwhile.

I am asked so often what I think about investing in New Zealand, or places further afield, and this is what I think:

- We are not short of good positive cash flow properties in Australia.

- To invest in New Zealand, you must set up a trust or a 'loss attributing qualifying company' (unique to New

Zealand). You must pay tax in New Zealand on any gain. You must borrow from a New Zealand bank.

- You cannot use your property here in Australia to cross-collateralise and this will limit your leveraging ability.

- Investing rules in New Zealand and other countries are very different than Australia's and you would need to learn about them before going ahead.

- And lastly, perhaps most importantly, why would you ever wish to send your money offshore? Show some patriotism and put your money back into this wonderful country of ours. I like New Zealand people but I don't want to give them my money, just as I would not expect them to want to give us theirs!

Stay in your own backyard, where you can maintain some control and become educated and smart about what you can do here on your own shores.

Investment clubs

If ever a scam could be cleverly disguised, the 'investment club' is perhaps one of the best. While the disingenuous nature of many seminars, workshops and wealth programs seems pretty obvious to some people, and it can be easy to stay away from the clutches of the sharks who run them (you just don't go along), 'investment clubs' have begun to spring up around the country using a carefully cultivated approach that trades on the Aussie need to congregate and be 'mates'.

On the surface, these clubs appear to be a group of your peers, working voluntarily for the good of all members to ensure that good 'Aussie battlers' are given a fair go in the property-investing world. In reality, this is a cover for an intricate network of seasoned con artists who use the club as a front for their own money-making adventures and a fence to sell overpriced and overvalued real estate to the unsuspecting public.

The head 'gurus' of groups such as this welcome devotees with promises of friendship, freedom and financial success through peer support and group effort. They tell you that they are there to help, free of charge, any time you need it. The warm and fuzzies continue through group meetings where friendships are made and fellow investors help each other. And in all fairness, many of the members offering this support are in fact genuine in their concern—they themselves are unaware of the dishonest network of money-hungry opportunists who lurk in the shadows.

While these clubs may seem 'free' and independent, I caution you to question the impartiality of any group that charges a 'commission' on the sale of the properties it recommends. This is not just a standard real estate commission of around 2 per cent, either. Often, as much as 6 per cent of the purchase price is demanded, putting you—the investor—way behind the eight ball from day one.

Don't be taken in by the welcome grin of these clubs. They are not what they seem, their advice is subjective and they profit from every purchase you make with commissions way above acceptable levels as well as purchase prices above market value.

Contracts with a 'rebate'

An acquaintance of mine was last week telling me about the circumstances surrounding the sale of her home, for which she was seeking $260 000. She told me how the person who had made the offer to buy it had no deposit (and so, technically, could not borrow any money to proceed), and how this potential buyer had planned to get around this.

'The contract will list the purchase price as $300000,' she advised. 'With luck, the bank valuer will value it the same. In the back pages of the contract will be a clause giving the buyer a $40000 rebate upon settlement. This way, she can borrow 90 per cent of the purchase price from the bank ($270000) and still have the $10000 left over to pay her costs.'

'But that's illegal!' I told her.

'Oh, but I won't know about it,' she said. 'The front page states a purchase price of $300000 and that is the price. It's not actually illegal, we are just giving her a rebate.'

I went on to explain to her that, as the vendor, she needed to sign this contract. When you sign a contract you must read it and you sign to attest to the fact that you have done so and agree to the conditions therein.

This meant that she would be agreeing to the rebate and would have full knowledge that the bank would be mislead into thinking she was charging the full $300000 for the property. As far as I could tell, this made her guilty of misleading and deceptive conduct (section 52 of the *Trade Practices Act*), and probably of mortgage fraud too, as she was withholding material information from the bank.

While having a rebate clause in the back of a contract is not illegal per se, the acts that it inspires certainly are! This person's attitude was unfortunate and, sadly, many people feel the same way—if you can get away with swindling the bank, that's fine because everyone, except the bank, wins.

Be very careful that any action you take when purchasing any property is transparent and you are very sure it is within the law. This includes making false representations to the bank about what you can afford to repay and taking out 'lo doc' loans (loans that require you to simply sign a statutory declaration as to your ability to repay), in which you lie about your earnings.

Becoming wealthy in retirement is simply not worth it if you have to do anything other than act with honesty and integrity. I'd rather be poor and honest than rich and dishonest, any day.

Land banking

Recently, an unscrupulous lot from overseas visited our shores and did their level best to leave with a handful of hard-earned cash from well-meaning investors. These particular charlatans were offering plots of land in Europe at ridiculously low prices. The catch? As yet, the plots had no planning permission, but the reassurance from the spruikers peddling these wares was that planning permission was around two years away. At that time, the values would skyrocket and the clever few who bought today would see instant wealth.

I was at an expo when I heard that these people were displaying beautifully presented plans of the sites, all nicely numbered and ready to be purchased. I was later told that the sites themselves didn't even exist yet, in fact subdivision had not even been approved, and, according to the locals, planning permission was not expected at all, at least not for the next 50 years.

These people were exhibitors and that morning they had been visited by the authorities who were not happy about a number of their practices. Later that day, I visited their stand myself and spoke to the head spruiker, who was flabbergasted that a representative from the authorities was concerned that he was quoting future expected returns of more than 600 per cent to potential buyers.

'I haven't said a word about expected returns,' he fumed. 'But in truth, all of our investors have seen more than 800 per cent return!'

The law had little clout to shut these people down, but thankfully they were made to cease trading on a small technicality relating to licensing. Since word has been passed around about these types of people, and there has been much written in the press and featured on TV, it seems they have been laying low, for the time being at least.

Land banking in general can make sense, if you are able to buy land with every chance of future planning approval and you can afford the high costs of holding an asset that does not generate income for you. However, the strategy becomes incredibly risky when you look overseas for land that you cannot confirm a future for.

Always take care and be very wary about anything that is presented to you with any dubious or difficult to confirm information. These people had lovely brochures and a great stand, but a little research would have uncovered the chequered past of the proprietors and alerted potential buyers to the fact that something was just not right.

Two-tier marketing

Two-tier marketing was banned in Queensland some years ago, but it doesn't mean it no longer happens. Of course it does!

In its most basic form, two-tier marketing involves the sale of property to out-of-towners at a price higher than what the same property would be sold to the locals for. While it can happen anywhere, it is most prolific in Queensland.

There are many variations on the theme of how property such as this is actually sold, but generally a marketer will target buyers from other states, either through telemarketing or through advertising. Often the potential buyers are offered a flight to sunny Queensland and a stay in a swank hotel, during which time they are courted and shown property that is well above market price. To prevent the buyer from asking too many questions, a 'one-stop shop' is set up, whereby each door in a suite of offices results in another step in the purchase being made. Buyers start in the sales office, then proceed to the accountant's office for financial advice, then on to the solicitor's office to sign a contract in which the cooling off period has been waived.

By the time the buyer reaches home shores, they are signed, sealed and delivered, and the discovery that the price was too high often comes way too late.

You do not necessarily need to view a property before you buy it for it to work for you, but you do need to take time to carry out the research. Never forget the 20 must-ask questions, which will go some way to ensuring that many of the problems that can arise from both this scheme and the others mentioned here do not happen to you.

More than one company

Remember Maurie, from chapter 1? He was so keen to accelerate what I considered to be an already well-progressing property investment strategy that he attended a 'masterclass' conducted by a spruiker who has been subject to ASIC enquiries. He wanted me to assist him in employing a strategy he had learned at the workshop.

Basically, he had been told that he should start by setting up a company in order to buy property. No doubt, an endless array of benefits in adopting this approach had been paraded before him, while the considerable drawbacks would have been glossed over.

The advice that really worried me, however, was that given to Maurie to counter the problem of reaching your borrowing limit with the bank.

You see, at some time, you may well reach your maximum borrowing capacity and, despite having increasing equity, your bank may not agree to lend you any more money (this is covered in greater depth in the following chapter).

At the masterclass, Maurie was told that this was a simple issue to get around. 'Just set up a new company,' he was told. This way, the commitments of the other company that had so far made all of the property purchases would not be considered by the bank, and the new company, having no commitments, could freely borrow.

This is simply rubbish. When you borrow from a bank, it will perform a director's search on you, which will reveal if you are the director of any other company. If you are, you will be asked to prove that the other company(s) does not have an unmanaged debt, and the commitments, income and expenses of all companies of which you are a director will be considered when ascertaining your borrowing capacity. So, not only does this particular strategy mean that you now have the cost of setting up and maintaining another company, it also does nothing to change your borrowing status!

Unfortunately, Maurie paid good money to hear such blatant garbage. In fact, in my opinion, nothing that Maurie told me he brought away from 'masterclass' was any use to him whatsoever! Hopefully there was *some* information in there that made his large investment worthwhile to him.

Summary

- Be very wary of investment seminars and thoroughly check out the company and the presenters before going along.

- Wrapping is a strategy that has had bad reviews and in my opinion, is somewhat immoral.

- Renovation takes time and effort and you rarely see a considerably increased value for these efforts.

- Buying off the plan can be incredibly dangerous and has resulted in many people losing money.

- Rent guarantees are not worth the paper they are written on and often mask underlying true returns.

- Buying overseas is complicated and unnecessary, as we have plenty of opportunities available within Australia.

- Investment clubs are often fronts for unscrupulous opportunists.

- Contracts that lie about the true purchase price by offering rebates to purchasers may well be breaking several laws.

- Land banking is a costly strategy and, when it involves overseas purchases, is highly risky.

- Two-tier marketing still exists and you should be very wary about any marketer who is willing to fly you to other states to buy his or her property.

- You cannot set up companies to enhance your borrowing capacity, as the bank considers all of the commitments of the borrowers, including commitments to company structures.

Conclusion

So often, people go along to seminars or consider risky strategies or ventures despite the fact that information about the dodgy practices of the people offering them is freely available on the internet or through the press.

In the words of Neil Jenman, a man whose opinion I respect enormously, 'don't sign anything' until you are very sure. Taken one step further, simply don't sign anything, especially on the first day you see it. Ensure you have good quality legal advice that you have found for yourself (not advice that has been provided by lawyers from the other side), and do an abundance of research. Be sure to always visit Neil's website at www.jenman. com.au and perform a search on anyone you are considering doing business with. Although the site it is not exhaustive, Neil has done some great work on uncovering many 'bad guys' over the years and some of them are featured in his many consumer alert articles.

Millions in minutes

_____

Slow and steady

I know of people who have been told about strategies in which you can become a 'millionaire' in four months, or amass property worth $10 million in 18 months, or otherwise obtain seemingly impossible numbers of properties in record-quick time.

Not only are these things simply not possible, they are also not necessary. You do not need anywhere near that much property to ensure a safe and secure retirement and all these people are doing is making most of the population feel that they will never achieve what they need to take care of their own retirement needs. The end result is that, often, people who have every chance of buying investment property instead feel that the requirements are too great and so they do nothing.

I am not suggesting that it is wrong to work toward a time when you are considered financially successful—many people want that and look far and wide for the idea or opportunity that will make this possible. However, there are an equal number of people who do not want untold riches—they simply want to be sure that their retirement years are fun and carefree and that they do not have to experience the money worries that many of us saw our parents suffer when they retired with little more than the age pension.

The main purpose of this book is to explode many of the untruths that are circulating about property. I am hoping that, so far, you have seen that there really is no such thing as a free lunch and that 95 per cent of what you hear will be sensationalist rubbish that, in the main, has no practical application.

Now, I would like to show you how anyone really can build a portfolio of properties, slowly, surely—but ultimately successfully, without having to know any secret or magic formula. Once you can see what you can achieve given some time and hard work, you can then begin to make your own future a little rosier. And, for those of you who want more than just a secure retirement, you will be able to see the additional work you can do with the same strategy to create even more success.

Risk

It is crucial that I take this opportunity to talk to you about risk. This is the one thing you never seem to hear about when you go to a seminar or read more about the latest get rich quick scheme. You hear about riches, results and return, but no-one ever talks about *risk*.

If you were to visit to a financial adviser to seek some guidance on where to invest, the very first thing he or she will do is complete your risk profile. A risk profile is a long list of questions that allows the adviser to determine where you sit on the risk scale. The results of the profile fall somewhere between being 'risk averse' and 'embracing risk'.

Why does the adviser do this? Simply because different investments carry with them different levels of risk and this in turn will indicate the level of return you can expect to receive.

Ever heard anyone claim that you can receive a huge return on a particular investment, without any risk? This is simply not true, and while people can and do invest in vehicles every day that give them a stunning return, it will not have been without a large degree of risk, which paid off for them this time but could have also resulted in total loss.

In relation to property, 'risk' refers to the chance that you will not see a suitable return in terms of the rental income, and/or the chance that you will not see suitable growth to have made the investment worthwhile. When people invest in property, rarely does the 'adviser' or 'agent' even talk about this risk. The outlook for property is always seen as rosy and people mistakenly believe that it is a no-risk strategy that always works out in the end. I have personally seen people buying property that was extremely high risk, and consequently lose a substantial amount of money when the results they were led to expect did not materialise.

I believe that if you are going to be a property investor, there are two things you must do. Firstly, you must understand your own risk profile, so that you know the level of risk you can tolerate. Then you must learn that different types of property carry different levels of risk. It will be vital for you to ensure that you seek out and purchase only those properties which match your risk profile.

Your property risk profile

You may have had a risk profile prepared for you by a financial adviser in the past and it should have highlighted the asset classes that most suit your personal attitude to risk.

A property risk profile is somewhat different. It takes into account that you have already made the conscious decision that *property* is the asset class in which you want to invest. It does not tell you whether you should invest in property or not, rather it helps you determine the *type* of property you should invest in, once you have already made the decision that property is going to be your investment vehicle of choice.

Josh and Marie were long-term clients of ours and we had assisted them in reducing the term of their personal mortgages. They had been along to a lot of seminars I had conducted and really wanted to invest in property, but each time they got close, Marie would get a headache and call the whole thing off. One day, I met with them to find out what was happening. After asking a lot of questions, it seemed to me that having worked hard to pay off their own home, Marie was reluctant to get into debt again. She had been looking at properties with values upwards of $250 000 and this seemed like a large amount to bite off.

I helped them to see that they did not need to start with such a high value property—at the time there was an abundance of options well below the $100 000 mark. Marie quickly found a two-bedroom townhouse in an outer suburb of Brisbane for just $79 000, and the sale went off without a hitch. Since then they have purchased six more properties, none of them of great value, and all of their properties are growing well and returning an income to them.

They had to recognise that their personal risk profile was that of very cautious investors, so they needed to look for the cheaper, 'bread-and-butter' properties that they could access at a low price and that they could be sure were in good demand as a rental.

In appendix B at the back of this book, I have included a personal risk profile that you can complete to determine your level of risk as it applies to property. Be sure to complete this profile before you commence your property investing so that you can ascertain the type of property that best matches your personal risk profile. After completing your profile, check chapter 3 in *How to Create an Income for Life* for a detailed analysis of all of the different property types available. There you will also find a risk rating for each different type to make it easier for you to choose.

At my last seminar, a participant told me that, since commercial property delivered a higher rent return than residential property, we should all be buying commercial property to maximise our returns. What he neglected to understand was that while the returns are certainly much greater, so are the risks. If someone with a 'risk averse' profile was to invest in commercial property, the stress and worry they would suffer would make this investment simply not worth it.

My husband and I own a few commercial offices, one of which we rent to our company, Destiny® Financial Solutions. There are 20 units in the complex, and, of the 20, five of them are owner-occupied and have been since the building was completed some two years ago. Of the other 15 units, 14 of them have been vacant since the day they were completed. This means that those people who had purchased these units as an investment have received no income for two years. As the purchase price was quite high, this is a long time to be without income and for those who borrowed to invest, I am certain they will be feeling financial stress, as is evidenced by the 'for sale' signs that are now prominent in a few of the units. The complex is very professional and the outlook prior to the completion was a positive one — the expectations were for a high demand due to the location in a growing business park, in the centre of a thriving community. The main problem is that there is an abundance of these units, with more being built every day, and so the competition is still too great for an investment like this to pay off just yet.

Some people could manage this type of risk and be able to stay in the market throughout these lean times, but others would either suffer severe financial distress, or feel so personally stressed by the situation that it impacts on their whole life. You must match your own risk profile to the risk rating of the different types of property available, and only choose to invest in property from your personal profile. Then, as you become more experienced at investing, complete a new profile to see if it has changed.

While *How to Create an Income for Life* has in-depth details on risk ratings for each type of property, below is a summary of risk as it relates to property and the type of properties that may be contained in each category.

Risk categories

Low risk

Property in the low-risk category includes residential property with a demonstrated tenancy history, in areas with a growing population close to or in a city or large regional area. It will be the type of property that attracts long-term renters, and is most probably in the lower third of the market in terms of value. This factor will make the property easier to liquidate in the event that you need to realise your capital quickly.

Examples of this type of property include houses and units in large towns or cities, which are let out on standard residential leases.

Medium risk

Property in the medium-risk category includes residential property in towns with an itinerant population or those areas based around one main industry. It may also include holiday rentals (not hotels or serviced apartments) in very well-established holiday areas that have a good history of tenancy and a strong return in the high season.

Examples of this type of property include houses or units in mining or small towns, and houses or units that are let out on a week to week basis during holiday periods or weekends.

High risk

Property in the high-risk category includes commercial, industrial and retail property as well as 'niche market' properties (that is, properties built for specific purposes). These properties have a high risk as tenure of tenancy cannot be guaranteed and history has shown that many of them suffer long periods of vacancy and difficulty attracting tenants.

Examples of this type of property include offices, warehouses, factories, shops and holiday rentals with on-site managers or hotel operators, as well as niche market property such as hotels, serviced apartments, retirement units and student accommodation.

'No-risk' property

The reason why there is not a category for no-risk property is because there is no such thing. Every time you make any investment, you take the risk that it will not work out for you and you will suffer a loss. The only way to prevent this risk is to not invest at all.

When my father was alive, he used to express concern that I would borrow to invest, and worried that there would come a time when it would all 'fall over' and I would be left with nothing.

I told him that I figured I could look at life two ways. I could do nothing and be afraid of the risk, and the absolute 100 per cent guarantee of this approach was that I would get nowhere and have nothing for my retirement years. Or, I could try my best and do what I could. The outcome of the latter approach would be one of two things. I would either get nothing and go nowhere, in which case I would be in the same position that I would have been in had I done nothing. Or, I would achieve what I wanted, and see my goals realised.

You cannot remove risk. You can, however, manage it and reduce the chances that you will suffer loss by ensuring that you have adequate insurance cover in place (see *How to Create an Income for Life*, chapter 8), and by being diligent in your research. The 20 must-ask questions are a crucial risk management tool.

How many properties do you need?

In previous chapters, I discussed how property can give you a positive cash flow and how having this cash flow can ensure that you build, and hold on to, a more substantial portfolio than you could if you were to choose properties with a negative cash flow. In order for you to know how many properties you need to accumulate to satisfy your retirement goals, you can start with some simple forward calculations. To calculate a forward retirement income, you need to choose a few variables.

I always like to assume that, in the main, an investment with a relatively stable potential for return can provide you with a return on capital of around 5 per cent. At present, the cash rate is around this amount and, at the very least, if you invested a lump sum in a term deposit (which is at call) with a major bank, you would see a return somewhere in the 5 per cent range. An investment such as this would not, however, show capital growth — the 5 per cent would be income only.

Additionally, we can expect that the average property will return 5 per cent of its value as a yearly rent return. This takes into account those properties providing far less than this (in larger cities) and those providing more (in regional areas). In reality, anyone following the principles of positive cash flow investing will probably see *at least* 5 per cent in rent return on any property he or she has purchased, as well as growth over time.

So, let's assume that you spend the years you have left till retirement buying property that will provide you with a retirement income. Once you do retire, you will probably do one of two things — you will sell what you have, repay debt and invest the balance, probably in one of the safer options such as a term deposit (as outlined above). Or, you will continue to hold the property, in which case you will still have a debt, but since the value of the entire portfolio should have risen somewhat (with some properties not gaining much, some gaining an average amount and some gaining a great deal), the difference between the values at that time and what you owe represents what you *own*. The 5 per cent rent return on the portion you own becomes income to you.

To formulate a starting point from which you can set some goals, you should first consider how much income you want to have in order to retire comfortably. Once you know this, you can then work out either how many properties (or what value of properties) you need to acquire, or how long it will be until you can leave the paid workforce. The example overleaf illustrates this.

income /09, 000

Sarah has decided that she would like an income of $50 000 in order to retire. At 5 per cent return (either on a lump sum invested or on the portion of her properties she can expect to own at that time), she will require property equity of $1 000 000 to supply her with this income.

Sarah wants to know how long it will take for a property portfolio to accumulate $1 000 000 in equity. To work it out, she assumes a capital growth rate of 5 per cent per annum and a rent return rate also of 5 per cent.

Sarah has $200 000 equity in her own home and so she is ready to get started. If she was to purchase 10 properties with a value of $150 000 each over the first five years, buying one at the start and then one every six months, and they each grew by 5 per cent per annum, she would have $1 725 400 worth of property at the end of the fifth year. Her total investment would be $1 575 000 (the purchase prices plus all of the costs to buy).

If she was to then hold on to what she had acquired and wait for time to do its work, and apply a growth factor of 5 per cent per annum, it would take a further nine-and-a-half years for her to have the $1 000 000 in equity she needs. The total time taken for her to create this retirement income has been 14-and-a-half years.

From this point, Sarah can manipulate the figures to determine other possible outcomes. For example, if growth was 6 per cent per annum instead of 5 per cent per annum, then she would achieve her goals one-and-a-half years sooner. If she was an aggressive investor, she might buy more property, sooner (the $200 000 equity would actually give her enough, subject to her satisfying bank lending criteria, to purchase almost $1 000 000 worth of property immediately, taking more time off her target). Otherwise, she could consider selling the portfolio and investing it in higher risk, higher return assets that may bring 8 to 10 per cent in income (although capital gains tax could alter the outcome of this option).

Ted and Janet only have eight years until Ted retires. They want to know how much they can expect to achieve in that time. They have $250 000 equity in their own home, which allows them to purchase around $1 200 000 worth of property immediately. For the first three years they are able to add $300 000 more property (as the growth has provided enough equity for this). Therefore, after three years, they have property valued at $2 334 900 (the original values growing at 5 per cent, multiplied by the number of years held so far) for a purchase price of $2 175 000 (including costs).

Assuming they buy no more at this stage (which is unlikely), the value of the portfolio by the eighth year will be $2 979 989. The potential income after eight years is an extra $40 200 more than they could have received had they done nothing at all. In joint names, this amount would still allow them to access much of the pension and so they now have the chance to accrue a more reasonable retirement income.

Remember, Sarah, and Ted and Janet still own the investments even after they have ceased working, and they will continue to grow and bring increasing income as the rents are increased over time. In addition, it is likely that neither of them will stop investing while they are still in the paid workforce, and both will probably use a rapid mortgage reduction system to repay debt sooner, so the real results would be considerably better than illustrated here. Later in this chapter, I will illustrate what can be achieved in a 15-year period by providing some examples of projections we have done for real clients of varying income levels and home equity.

It is an important part of your investing strategy to set some kind of retirement income goal that can then determine how much property you need to accumulate to enable you to leave the paid workforce. This way, you will have guidelines and motivation as you strive to achieve the goals you have set. All of the clients we have assisted have as their starting point a projection that shows them what they could achieve given what we know about their income, expenses, home equity and potential borrowing capacities. Having this plan not only provides an excellent blueprint for them — with us as mentors it also helps them to stay on track and commit to their goals.

Buy, build and snowball

After we had been investing for around six years, my husband and I sat down and contemplated where we were at. It had seemed during those six years that all we were doing was taking one step forward and then, almost, another back again. Each time we had realised equity in our portfolio, we had borrowed and bought again, and, often due to purchase costs, it seemed to make an instant hole in our progress. We were always increasing our borrowings to 80 per cent of what we owned and, while our portfolio was small, it seemed that the 20 per cent we *did* own wasn't growing that much.

We *had* started with only $80 000 equity in our own home, and at that point we had about $3 million in property and about $2.2 million in debt, so in reality we had already increased the portion we owned tenfold. However, it still seemed as though we were not moving fast enough, given that six years had already passed. As I am somewhat impatient, I started thinking that the whole thing was progressing too slowly—safely, yes, but definitely slowly!

Being 42 at the time, I figured that I had about 10 years more that I wanted to work, so I did some calculations on the position we would be in 10 years hence, based on the property we had already acquired.

At that moment in time, we had $3 million worth of property. We owned just $800 000 worth, or enough to create an income of around $40 000 per annum. If we did nothing more from that moment (highly unlikely) and if property did *not* double in the following 10 years, but increased its value by only half, then in the next 10 years we would own $4 500 000 worth of property. If we paid *nothing* off the debt from that point (highly unlikely also as the cash flows alone were making principal repayments for us), the debt would still be $2.2 million. The amount of property we *owned* would be $2.3 million and at a 5 per cent return, that would equal a $115 000 per annum income.

We needed to do nothing more from that point and we could still create a passive income of $115 000 per annum by the time I was 52! And, of course, the possibilities are probably even better than that. If some of those properties *do* double in that 10-year period, the results will be far more impressive. If we can get more than 5 per cent in growth and/or income, the results will also be greater. And, if we continue to buy more property (which we have), then the possibilities are actually *much* better than $115 000 per annum.

We have just purchased the property that has increased the value of our portfolio to well over $6 million. Even if we owed $6 million (which we don't), a 6 per cent growth on this portfolio every year for the next 10 years would result in a portfolio worth $10.7 million. The $4.7 million equity would result in an income over $235 000 per annum and, since we don't have $6 million in debt, our actual income is going to be closer to $300 000 per annum. And that, I feel, is the *least* we can expect.

So, now to the point. In the first five to seven years, it may seem like not too much is happening (although, as you can see from above, even in that period of time you can make a difference). It will be made to look worse by the blatant claims of property 'gurus' who shamelessly spruik the ability to buy and then profit from millions of dollars of property in seemingly short periods of time. You will wonder why your own portfolio is creeping along at a snail's pace while the property world is screaming of immediate riches.

However, just when the believers of all the hype are realising that the strategies are flawed, and just when the hawkers of dubious success are appearing in our courts being charged with misleading and deceptive conduct and an array of other crimes, your portfolio will begin to hit its straps and take off for you.

It is exactly like the hare and the tortoise. I promise you that with hard work, perseverance and patience, your slow and measured approach to building your portfolio *will* pay off. Time is the key and an extra five years can make a huge difference to the final outcome.

Rapid mortgage reduction and positive cash flow property

In previous chapters, I have discussed the importance of using rapid mortgage reduction for your personal, and then your investment, debt. *How to Make Your Money Last as Long as You Do* (chapter 5) and *How to Create an Income for Life* (chapter 9) both have complete details on exactly how to set up a mortgage reduction plan.

I have also discussed the importance of allowing all of the extra cash flow you make from your investment property to flow through your debts, no matter how small that cash flow is. This is not only because you will offset interest by making these additional repayments, but, if you also leave the cash flow in your debt permanently, you will pay off additional principal and so reduce the term of your debt even further.

When we at Destiny® show people how to pay off their personal mortgages earlier, we do so by instructing them to ensure all income from all sources flows through their mortgages, and that they only ever re-draw enough to meet personal, budgeted expenses. This will have the joint result of offsetting interest *and* repaying principal, and so, naturally, the loan will be finalised much sooner.

When you buy negatively geared property, you have a commitment to the property in order to make up the shortfall between income and expenses. Tax breaks on your loss will provide you with some money to do this, but since the most you can ever get back is 45 cents in every lost dollar (subject to your own personal marginal rate of tax), you must find the rest. This means that you will need to access any surplus personal funds you have, and therefore have less available funds to make extra repayments into your personal mortgage. Owning negative cash flow property then results in you taking longer to repay your debts, as you have less money available for extra repayments.

Anyone who uses rapid mortgage reduction *and* buys positive cash flow property has *more* funds available, and if he or she is committed enough to pay this into his or her debts, it will speed up the process of debt repayment.

Do you recall something I stated earlier in this book?

> *For every $1 of debt you repay, that's $5 more property you can buy through borrowing.*

So it follows that, if you are able to speed up debt repayment, and thus increase equity, you will also speed up property acquisition, and so your exposure to growth assets. All in all, the snowballing effect of all of this means that you will benefit from more than just the interest savings on the debt you are reducing more quickly.

Real people

I would like to tell you about some real people we have helped to start out on their own retirement plans. Of course, I will change the names but I am going to use all of their information, exactly as they gave it to us. This way, you can see what is possible for investors, given a range of different personal circumstances.

The illustrations I have chosen will assume a number of things about all of the clients:

1.   The clients had no current investment properties.

2.   They had their own home, with a mortgage.

3.   They had an income that the bank would accept for borrowing purposes. The projections we did included an analysis on their borrowing capacities, so we knew that the bank would allow them to buy at least the number of properties we forecast for them.

4.   We used a 6 per cent per annum growth rate on property, and also increased income and expenses by an inflation rate of 3 per cent.

5.   We only forecast the purchase of 10 properties, but then carried the projection out to 15 years. So, after 10 properties were acquired, the clients then sat on these and allowed growth to do its work. In reality, they would probably continue to buy and this would enhance the results further.

6.   The clients committed to using the system provided to them, which required that they use rapid mortgage reduction and follow the financial management system available exclusively to our clients. This ensures that they track not only their budgets, but also their property portfolios and so can supervise the outcome more efficiently.

7. The 'possible retirement income' displayed is a result
   of taking total property values at the end of the 15
   years, taking off the value of the personal home and the
   remaining debt and multiplying the results by 5 per cent
   (rent return).

8. All projections used 'sample' properties to make the
   forecast. The samples used were actual properties for
   which we were able to obtain purchase prices, costs and
   full depreciation schedules.

9. Properties were added to the portfolio every time equity
   and loan serviceability allowed, up to a maximum of 10
   properties.

Dean and Sue

*Dean and Sue were 37 and 34 years of age. Their
financial circumstances were as follows:*

Incomes:	$33438 and $12536
Home value:	$390000
Debt:	$225000
Net worth:	$165000
Monthly expenses:	$3730
Monthly surplus:	$85
Current remaining term on debt:	22.1 years

*After projecting positive cash flow property
purchases valued at $145000 each, Dean and Sue's
results are:*

New personal debt loan term: 9.12 years

(cont'd overleaf)

(cont'd)

Properties purchased:

2 in the first 12 months, then:

month 23

month 37

month 53

month 65

month 76

month 84

month 95

month 101

Net worth of investment properties after 15 years:	$1 398 000
Possible monthly retirement income after 15 years:	$5 825

might not be enough after 15 years due to inflation!

In the case of Dean and Sue, they only had $85 a month available after meeting personal expenses, and they have still managed to create an income of $70 000 a year.

Joel

Joel is 42. His financial circumstances were as follows:

Income:	$68 983
Home value:	$300 000
Debt:	$131 629
Net worth:	$168 371
Monthly expenses:	$4 555

Monthly surplus: $107

Current remaining term on debt: 17 years

After projecting positive cash flow property purchases valued at $175000 each, Joel's results are:

New personal debt loan term: 4.25 years

Properties purchased:

4 in the first 12 months, then:

month 23

month 27

month 35

month 46

month 56

month 66

Net worth of investment
properties after 15 years: $2256960

Possible monthly retirement
income after 15 years: $9404

In the case of Joel, he had $107 a month available after meeting personal expenses, and he has still managed to create an income of $112848 a year.

John and James

John is 39 and James is 40. Their financial circumstances were as follows:

Incomes: $132318 and $33875

Home value: $1250000

(cont'd overleaf)

(cont'd)

Debt:	$239945
Net worth:	$1010055
Monthly expenses:	$9961
Monthly surplus:	$1091
Current remaining term on debt:	25.75 years

After projecting positive cash flow property purchases valued at $245000 each, John and James' results are:

New personal debt loan term:	2.58 years

Properties purchased:

8 in the first 12 months, then:

month 13

month 19

Net worth of investment properties after 15 years:	$2496480
Possible monthly retirement income after 15 years:	$10402.41

In the case of John and James, they had sufficient equity to purchase property very quickly, subsequent to which they sat with these properties and let time do its work. In reality it is far more likely that they will continue to buy for at least a few more years, which will have an impact on the final outcome.

It doesn't matter what your income, you can still not only undertake rapid mortgage reduction, but also put in place a property strategy that will make *some* change to your circumstances. I am often approached by people who tell me that they are in their mid- to late-50s and that, obviously, it is too late for them.

Even if they could only generate an extra $10000 a year in income, surely that is better than not doing anything at all. In doing so, they would have acquired growth assets that can continue to grow in value and increase this income amount for every year that they are retired.

It's never too late to begin. You simply need an income, and a small amount of equity in a property somewhere. Then you are ready to get started.

How leverage works

I have covered the topic of leveraging in great detail in almost all of my books, and still it has a place in this one. People are often confused as to how the entire strategy comes together, of how equity essentially equals property deposits and how the loan structure should be designed.

For this illustration, I will take a very basic portfolio and demonstrate how each property is added and what the resulting loan looks like. The illustration will assume that the investor always borrows 80 per cent of the total values of the properties. I will also consider 6 per cent as a growth rate and that no reduction to any of the principals is ever made, which of course would not happen in real life. Please refer to my other books in order to see more detail on this process.

Step 1

Own home of $250 000, debt $150 000

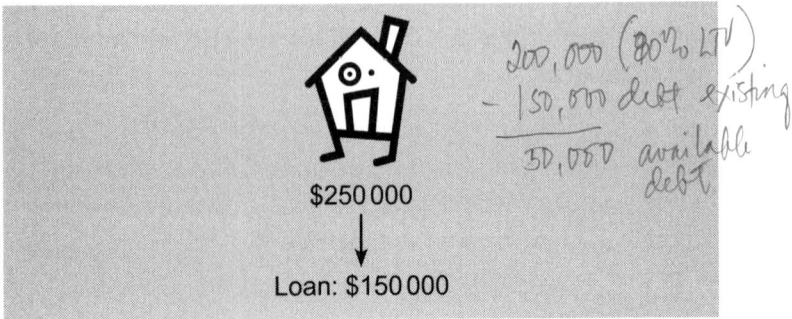

$250 000

Loan: $150 000

In reality, the bank would lend this person $200 000, based on the value of the property at 80 per cent, assuming he or she could service the debt according to bank lending criteria. This means that $50 000 is available to make another purchase. Imagining that purchasing costs are $10 000, this leaves $40 000 to buy another property. At the ratio of a $4 loan for every $1 in equity, the new purchase could be $200 000—that is, $40 000 from the current equity and $160 000 from the new security property). The structure then looks like this:

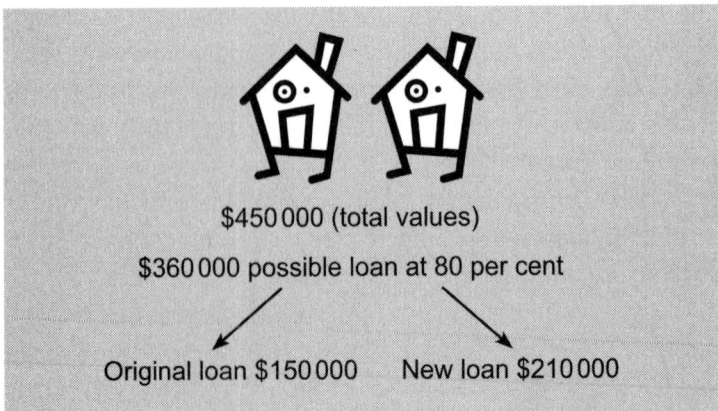

$450 000 (total values)

$360 000 possible loan at 80 per cent

Original loan $150 000   New loan $210 000

The $210 000 is enough to buy the new property and pay the costs.

Step 2

Two-and-a-half years go by. The properties are now worth $520 000. The equity has grown by $70 000. Again, assuming that the bank will lend 80 per cent of the total equity, and $10 000 of the increase is needed for costs, this person can afford to buy another property valued at $230 000. It looks like this:

① $520 (.80) = 416$
② $416 - 150 - 210 = 56$
③ $56 - 10 cost = 46$

④ $46 (5) = 230$
↑
1:5 purchasing
power for
p 155

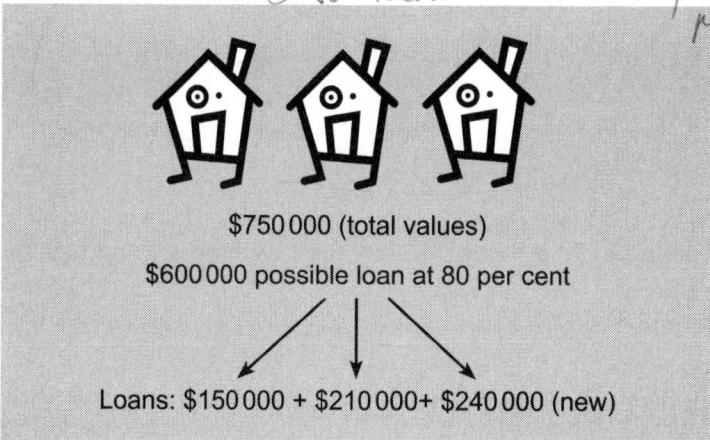

$750 000 (total values)

$600 000 possible loan at 80 per cent

Loans: $150 000 + $210 000 + $240 000 (new)

The $240 000 is enough to buy the new property and pay the costs.

Step 3

One-and-a-half more years pass. The properties are now worth $818 000. The equity has grown by a further $68 000. The person goes back to the bank and discovers that he or she can borrow a total of $654 400 on existing equity. Assuming

$10 000 purchasing costs, this person can afford to increase his or her loan and add another property valued at $222 000. It looks like this:

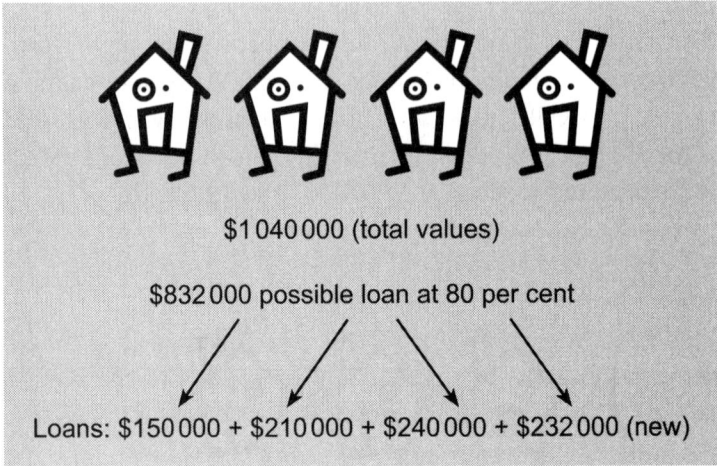

$1 040 000 (total values)

$832 000 possible loan at 80 per cent

Loans: $150 000 + $210 000 + $240 000 + $232 000 (new)

The $232 000 is enough to buy the new property and pay the costs.

Step 4

Let's take this just one step further. One more year passes. The properties are now worth $1 102 400. The equity has grown by a further $62 400. The person goes back to the bank and discovers that he or she could borrow a total of $881 920 on existing equity. Assuming $10 000 purchasing costs, this person can afford to buy another property valued at $199 600. It looks like this:

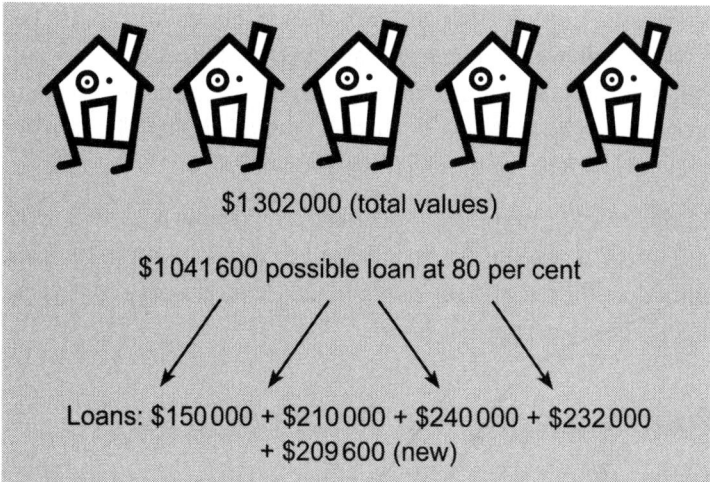

$1 302 000 (total values)

$1 041 600 possible loan at 80 per cent

Loans: $150 000 + $210 000 + $240 000 + $232 000
+ $209 600 (new)

The $209 600 is enough to buy the new property and pay the costs.

To summarise, five years have passed. The portfolio, originally containing one property at $250 000, now has five properties valued at $1 302 000. The net worth of the investor went from $100 000 to $260 400. Had he or she not invested at all and instead sat with just their own home rising in value, he or she would have only gained $84 500 in equity increase, and this equity would not have been able to generate an income for him or her. By buying the properties, the investor has more than tripled the potential growth in their net worth, and added $176 000 in income producing potential. In reality, they would also have paid off debt during this time, further increasing their net worth.

Notice also that the purchase of new property began to happen more quickly as the portfolio grew. I still recall when we bought our own home. It cost $370 000 and after one year, we had seen a 10 per cent growth, meaning that it was worth $37 000 more (enough to form a deposit on one small investment property).

Now, with our portfolio valued at over $6 million, a 10 per cent growth would mean we are worth $500 000 more, and this would be enough to form a deposit on around 12 more properties. The more exposure to a growth market, the quicker you can leverage again into more property.

All the investor in the example needs to do now is let time do a little more work and he or she can begin to buy property even more quickly, reaping the real benefits of increased growth that this kind of leverage can bring.

Positive gearing — to use or not to use

Earlier in the book, I talked about the very important differences between positive cash flow property and positively geared property.

Positive cash flow property is property where the income may be less than the expenses, but the shortfall is more than recouped because the property you have chosen has on-paper deductions — items that can be depreciated to result in a tax refund.

Positively geared property has income that is more than you need to pay the expenses. Although rare these days, it can be found, often in smaller regional areas, or where you are lucky enough to pick up a block of units or a group of more than one property for a price that is low because you bought them all.

The difference between these two can be important to know once you get to the point where your portfolio is growing, as the actual position of each new property (that is, which number they are) in your portfolio will affect its tax treatment.

You see, when you buy positive cash flow property, your total income (from rents and from any job you have) is reduced by the amount of the on-paper loss. It could be that when you begin you pay tax at the 45 per cent marginal rate, and then, after a few purchases, you are able to write off enough income to bring you down into the 40 per cent, then 30 per cent tax bracket. As you come down through the brackets, making a positive cash flow out of property is going to become harder and harder. A property with a $5000 on-paper loss will provide a tax refund of $2250 to someone in the highest bracket, $2000 to someone in the 40 per cent bracket, $1500 to a taxpayer in the 30 per cent bracket and only $750 to a person in the 15 per cent bracket. The lower the bracket, the more on-paper deductions you need to make up the shortfall between income and expenses.

In fact, a property you buy as a first property that provides a $15-a-week positive cash flow may only provide you with a $5-a-week cash flow if it is purchased as, say, your sixth property.

Alternatively, the lower your tax bracket, the more important it becomes to buy positively geared property where income is greater than expenses. If you are in a low tax bracket, you will want to find a property that requires very little in the way of on-paper deductions to make up the difference (so one where income is not too much lower than expenses) or one that has income greater than expenses, as happens with positively geared property. Remember, positively geared property is one on which you make a net gain and so you actually pay tax. People on lower incomes have a reduced marginal rate of tax and so only pay a low rate of tax on any gain they do make on property such as this.

The same can be said for anyone whose income has now been written down into the lower brackets as a result of consistent positive cash flow investing—once you have used up the bulk of your tax breaks in the higher brackets and you start to pay considerably less tax, you should begin seeking positively geared property, or positive cash flow property that only has a small negative gap between income and expenses.

Your portfolio will require careful planning. You must assess the cash flow of each new purchase according to where it sits in your portfolio, and what tax bracket you are in at the time. We make sure that any of our clients using the Destiny® System have access to the calculators they need to assess this, as it really can make a big difference to your overall cash flow if you do not accurately assess the individual cash flows.

Generally, you will need to buy positive cash flow property to begin with, until you are in the lower brackets. Then, for a time, you will need to buy positively geared property, as these will *add* to your net income and take you back up through the tax brackets again. Once you creep up, then more positive cash flow property is required.

Attention to detail and the ability to balance your portfolio in this way are important skills for all investors to have.

But the bank won't lend to me!

Sometimes when people consider their investing potential, they call the bank and ask how much they could borrow given their current salaries.

Often, they are disappointed to discover that their borrowing capacities seem to be far less than what they would need to put in place a sizeable portfolio.

In reality, every time you buy a new property, the rent that it makes is considered as the additional income upon which you can calculate your borrowing capacity. This means that, as you buy more property, your income increases and so does your ability to borrow. In addition to this, some banks will lend more to you than others will, and so it can be worth shopping around for the best deal.

In all of the examples I have given in this chapter, the personal borrowing capacity of all of the investors was considered when we did their projections for them. From what we know about current lending rules, all of our clients should be able to achieve the goals we set for them and should qualify for enough borrowings to buy property at the rate we have projected.

Houses or units?

Earlier in the chapter, I covered risk and pointed out that you should be buying the kind of property that most suits your risk profile. When I speak at expos, people always ask me whether it is better to buy units or houses. The general consensus of opinion is that a house will increase in value more than a unit as it has a greater land component.

In truth, I have not found any real evidence to support this theory. The type of property you should buy must depend on what your research has discovered about the area. For example, if I was buying property in Perth, then I would surely choose a house and land, where there are at least four bedrooms, two bathrooms and the abundance of living areas that seem so popular in that city. This is because these are the features that are most in demand and purchasing such a property would increase my chances of sustained tenancy. Conversely, in Mount Isa, the population is largely itinerant, with many of the miners who live in town maintaining a family home elsewhere, living in town only during the period of their weekly shift. These people want rental properties that are small and easy to care for, and in these situations I would choose a unit every time.

The differences in potential tax breaks will, as always, depend on the property itself, and should not be the first consideration you have when deciding which type to buy.

Property trading

Buying and selling property for quick profits requires an incredible amount of time and effort as well as an astuteness that many of us simply don't have. An element of being in the right place at the right time is also needed, and often we see people making big money from the quick turnaround of a property they were lucky enough to buy right at the beginning of a large boom.

To buy and sell property in this country is a costly exercise. It can take more than a year to recoup your buying costs and put yourself back on square one. In addition, selling property attracts capital gains tax, at the very least on half of the gain and, if sold within 12 months, on the full gain. Once you begin to buy and sell property prolifically, the tax office may treat you as a property trader and change your taxation arrangements. Liquidating your assets will most likely result in a realised gain, which you will need to invest elsewhere. As cash, the return this new investment makes will be taxable without the tax benefits the same amount was receiving as a geared amount, using borrowings for your property investing. The end result is likely to be somewhat less profitable for you.

The strategies I teach are slow, steady and need some time to deliver good results. They allow you to enjoy a higher level of safety while still achieving realistic ends. I am not a fan of property trading and caution anyone who wants to give this a go to be sure that they have both the time and the knowledge to make it work for them. I can't say I have met too many people who have made any real money from this exercise.

Summary

- You must commence your investing life by being sure you understand your personal risk profile.

- It is important to note that all properties will have a different level of risk and so suit different investors.

- There is no such thing as 'no-risk' property.

- You do not need hundreds or even dozens of properties to build a solid retirement income — time and hard work and 10 properties may well be enough for you.

- The power of leverage will increase your exposure to growth markets and so allow you to build your portfolio more quickly.

- Positive cash flow property can help speed up debt repayment.

- Your borrowing capacity will increase as you acquire income-producing assets.

- You must know when to buy positive cash flow property and when to buy positively geared property.

- You should not choose between units or houses based on what they are — rather, it should be based on your target market and what it demands.

- Property trading is time consuming and costly and rarely results in enough gain to make it worthwhile.

Conclusion

I have never really been a big risk-taker, preferring instead to take a slower approach where my risk is measured and my strategy planned and well thought out. Because of this, when we began our portfolio of properties, we were incredibly careful, buying bread-and-butter property without any expected stunning growth potential, knowing that at least it would always be in demand as a rental and it would be relatively easy to offload in the event that we needed to do so.

Now, I probably would take much greater risks, but I still like my property to be what I call 'very ordinary'—the type of property the average person might live in and is affordable to the greater majority of the market. It has worked so well for my husband and me in the past, and, interestingly enough, some of our choices have actually gone on to be stunning performers after all!

Don't try to rush things and, above all, don't try to make things too complicated. Resist the urge to be carried away by the wave of enthusiasm being produced by the property frenzy, and go about the job of investing with a cool head. It will most certainly pay off over the long term.

Chapter 9 _____

Tax and positive cash flow

_____

To claim or not to claim

I remember speaking to a gentleman who told me that he did not want to claim depreciation on any of his properties because he would only have to pay it back, and because he had to replace the items he was claiming at some time anyway.

This made no sense on two counts—firstly, you do not have to pay it back, *per se*, although there is an adjustment when and if you sell. Even with this adjustment, there is a strong case, as I will show you, for claiming the depreciation now, when you need the cash flow the most. The second reason it made no sense was because whether you claim the depreciation on an item or not, you still have to replace it at some time. Not claiming it does not suddenly give it an extended life!

I am not going to go into lengthy detail about tax and tax claims. *How to Create an Income for Life* has a detailed chapter (chapter 10) on all of the possible things you can and cannot claim, and *How to Maximise your Property Portfolio* (chapter 5) takes this one step further by explaining concepts such as actual depreciation methods and low-value pooling. For those readers who want to be sure that they are very familiar with tax, these sections are a must-read.

I will, however, summarise tax claims for property investors to give you some idea of what you are doing and what you need to look out for when buying property.

Property and tax claims

When you purchase an income-producing asset, you are allowed to make a claim for the up-front, the ongoing and the selling costs of the investment. This is provided to encourage us to invest for our futures, and, where housing is concerned, to encourage private landlords who provide the bulk of the rental accommodation needed for the almost 25 per cent of the population who do not own their home. When it is suggested to me that the government will one day remove the gearing benefits it provides to investors of property, I can't help but wonder how it could do this and then expect to house the millions of people who would become displaced as private landlords sold up all over the country. I read recently that, at present, the government is providing around 3 to 4 per cent of the total rental housing, meaning that over 20 per cent is provided privately. I am inclined to believe that the government simply could not afford such a crisis.

The way you claim your benefits depends on the item you wish to claim, how you came by it and how you earn income other than any rents you receive.

When you buy property as an investment, the rent you receive will be tacked on to the top of any other income you earn. Before you are charged extra tax, however, you are allowed to deduct any costs you incur for holding the property. The resulting amount then becomes your new taxable income.

The items for which you may claim a tax deduction fall into different categories that determine how much you can claim and when you may make the claims.

Capital costs

The first type of cost you are likely to incur when you buy property will be known as 'capital costs'. These are the bulk of the <u>costs that arise from making the actual purchase or affecting a sale,</u> and include:

- any stamp duty you have paid to the state government on the purchase price (different in each state)

- any commissions or payments made to selling agents

- costs incurred by retaining a conveyancer or solicitor, such as search fees and the conveyancer's labour charge

- the cost of any improvements made to the property of a capital nature (that is, additions and renovations, not repairs)

- initial pest inspections and building inspections

- any other cost incurred in making the purchase or effecting the sale.

These items will not provide you with an immediate tax deduction, as you cannot claim them against your regular and rental income. Rather, <u>they are taken into account at the end of your holding period (that is, upon sale)</u> and when calculating your capital gain for tax purposes.

Jess bought a property worth $150 000. The total purchasing costs were $7250. While she owned the property, she spent $10 000 on a pergola. She sold this property 10 years later for $250000. In order to effect the sale, she paid $5000 commission to an agent and $1250 to a conveyancer.

The gain she made on the property of $100000 is reduced by the $23500 in costs she incurred, to $76500. This is the amount to be considered for capital gains tax calculations (see later section).

Revenue costs

When you own an investment property, you will incur an abundance of ongoing costs. Any cost that you incur in the process of earning an investment income can be claimed against that and any other income you earn to reduce the tax that you pay. Remember that an asset must be income-producing to attract these tax benefits—vacant land and collectibles would not qualify for these types of deductions, and nor will any property you own that is not a principal place of residence but that also does not earn an income (such as a holiday house). The following list includes some of the costs you may claim, although it is not an exhaustive list:

- interest on your investment loan, as long as the purpose for the amount you are claiming was purely investment

- interest on any loan taken out to purchase additional assets for the property, such as furniture, or for any loans taken out to effect repairs or carry out renovations or additions

- pest control and building maintenance, not including pre-purchase inspections

- water rates, council rates and all energy costs

- telephone charges

- property management fees, including letting costs, advertising costs, inspection fees and sundries

- body corporate fees

- quantity surveyor's costs

- owner's travel costs reasonably associated with twice-yearly inspections, not including those incurred for any holiday or other venture undertaken at the same time (so you cannot take a holiday and claim the costs of it if you happen to also carry out an inspection while you are there)

- land tax

- repair bills not relating to a renovation or addition or replacement of a capital asset (such as a hot water service)

- cleaning, gardening and property maintenance

- insurance, including building, contents, public liability and landlord's

- borrowing costs, including establishment fees, loan stamp duty, lender's mortgage insurance and valuation costs. Note, however that these must be claimed over a five-year period, or the period the investment is held, whichever is the shorter.

Each of these costs, except borrowing costs, must be claimed in the year in which they are incurred and, in essence, you receive a refund equivalent to your marginal rate of tax for every dollar claimed. So, a claim of $100 for gardening would result in tax benefits of 30¢ for someone in the 30 per cent tax bracket. The cost must have related in its entirety to the earning of the income, and it must have been paid by the person making the claim, who owns the asset. Where the property was not earning an income for a full year, a pro rata claim equal to the number of days on which it was earning an income can be made.

Depreciation

In addition to actual costs that you do incur, you may make a claim for the loss in value of many items relating to the actual property itself. Since the price you paid for the property included all of the things inside it and the building itself, you do not have to pay out any more money in order to make these claims. The tax office simply recognises that your asset becomes worth less (even though the property price rises) as it comes closer to needing replacement. Being able to make these claims gives you money that you can put away (back into your debt) until such times as you need to use it to make repairs or replace worn-out items.

Depreciation is divided into the following two categories.

Capital works deduction (division 43 allowance)

This refers to the claim you can make on the depreciating value of the building. The amount you may claim depends on the use of the property and the original construction date, and varies widely from property to property. This is covered in full in *How to Maximise Your Property Portfolio* (chapter 5) and also in *How to Create an Income for Life* (chapter 10). However, for the majority of investors whose residential property was built after 15 September 1987, the amount that may be claimed is 2.5 per cent of the original construction value, for a period of 40 years.

> Tash bought a property in 2004 that was originally built in 1993. She paid $220000 for the property, but was not sure how much she could claim on the division 43 allowance. She phoned a quantity surveyor and for $550 they prepared a report that gave her detailed information about the original costs of the building, as well as the

current value of all of the fixtures, fittings and furniture (see next section).

From this, she discovered that the original building had been erected for a cost of $118 000. She could now make a claim of $2950 every year for the remaining 29 years. Note she cannot claim any unclaimed depreciation from the former owners.

Capital works deductions considers all fixed items that are a part of the 'setting for income-producing activity' and some of the fees incurred, including:

- architect's fees, engineering and excavation costs
- retaining walls and fences
- all built-in cupboards and fixed items
- wiring, plumbing and gas fittings
- driveways and paths
- clothes hoists
- in-ground pools
- fixed tiling
- windows, shutters and roller doors
- sinks, tubs and toilet bowls
- doors, screens and skylights.

It does not include:

- the cost of the land or clearing the land
- landscaping
- builder's profit margin.

Plant and equipment (division 42 allowance)

Many income-producing properties also contain items that are part of the income producing activity, yet are not fixed. For all of these items, the owner may claim depreciation, at differing rates, depending on the item and its effective life. The effective life may be somewhere between one and 20 years, depending on the item.

The Australian Tax Office website (www.ato.gov.au) has available for download a list of all items that you can claim and suggested effective lives. If you have a genuine case for thinking that an item in your property has a different effective life than the one suggested by the commissioner, you may make a different claim, as long as you have evidence to back it up.

Some of the items that may be included in a property you buy are:

- furniture

- window treatments

- hot water services

- lawn mowers

- floor coverings

- whitegoods

- kitchen and other appliances

- washing machines and dryers.

Mostly, any item that can be removed or replaced will be considered to be part of the plant and equipment and so should be eligible for some type of claim.

The size of the claim you can make, and the way you can claim it, will depend on the item, its effective life and the best method of depreciation for your personal circumstances. Be sure to read

How to Maximise Your Property Portfolio (pages 85 to 86) as this will give you in-depth information about the different methods of depreciation, and how each method has a different impact on your cash flow over time.

Your quantity surveyor can establish for you the effective life of all of the plant and equipment in your property and he or she will include this as a part of his or her report.

What happens when depreciation runs out?

Usually, when looking for a property, you will perform calculations that will include an allocated amount that takes into account the potential depreciation. This is the only way you can work out whether there is a chance that the property will return a positive cash flow.

However, while division 43 lasts for 40 years (from original construction date), plant and equipment have nowhere near this life, with an average life of just five to seven years. It is highly likely that, while you own it, some of your tax deductibility will be reduced or perhaps even diminished completely.

It is important that you calculate not only how much depreciation you have available to you but also try to ascertain how it will diminish so that you can plan for this.

Since each and every item will have such a vast difference in the amount you can claim and the period over which you can claim it, there is no easy way to really work out the life of this depreciation. So, in my own portfolio, I usually plan on seven to 10 years of division 42 allowances.

You can start by isolating the building depreciation. On properties built after 1987, building depreciation lasts for 40 years, and if the property was not new when you purchased it, you may claim the balance of years remaining since the original construction date. You know that you have 40 years of this, or the balance of the depreciation, depending upon when the property was built. Most investors get at least 25 to 30 years of building depreciation and so this is an area you do not have to worry about too much.

Next, ascertain the cash flow again, using only the building depreciation and ignoring the plant and equipment allowances. Try to calculate how low the balance of the loan has to be in order for you to get a positive cash flow without needing the division 42 allowance to provide it. The following example illustrates this.

Imagine that your cash flow is going to be $10 a week positive and you have $3500 worth of on-paper deductions for the fixtures, fittings and furniture.

If you are in the 30 per cent tax bracket, this $3500 has given you $1050 of extra cash flow, or $20 a week. Without it, the cash flow of the property would be $10 a week negative.

You must work out what has to happen to see a positive cash flow, without the need to claim the division 42 allowances. In this instance, the property would need to have a $15 or so per week increase to the rent (as a $15 increase would attract tax of $5, leaving a net of $10), or the interest bill on your loan needs to go down by $10 a week ($520 a year). To achieve this, your loan balance would need to be $7428 (at 7 per cent) less.

So, you have to work toward ensuring that in the next seven years (the time in which many of your Division 42 allowances will be finalised), your loan balance has reduced by $7248 or the rents have had the chance to increase by $15, or a combination of both.

People who worry about depreciation running out are usually those who only pay the interest on their loans. If you undertake a rapid mortgage reduction strategy, you will repay debt faster and so prepare yourself for a time when the depreciation is no longer available to you.

Once you have a larger portfolio of properties, you should always look at the cash flow of the 'group' as a whole. This way, the importance of any one property to have a great cash flow is slightly diminished, and your properties can support each other. Just ensure that there is ample cash flow across the portfolio to provide the margin you need to manage those risks outlined earlier in the book (vacancy and rate rises), as well as the times when some of your properties begin to lose depreciation benefits.

Paying back depreciation

It's a myth that you have to pay back depreciation; however, you do have to make an adjustment for it upon sale. The facts are that, often, you may never reach the point where the adjustment has to be made at all—simply never sell and the issue will not arise.

But if you do, the amount of adjustment will never be as much as you have claimed along the way, and the benefits of having additional cash flow *now* that you can put straight back into your debt to create equity for quicker leveraging into more growth assets far outweighs the issue of making the adjustment in later years. Look at the two following examples.

Terry owns a property worth $200 000, which he kept for 10 years. He could have claimed approximate depreciation of $5000 per year, but he did not want to be in the position of making an adjustment upon sale.

He sold the property for $300 000, in effect incurring a gain of $100 000. His buying and selling costs were $14 000 and so his net gain was $86 000.

As Terry held this property for more than 12 months, he qualifies for discounted capital gains tax. He pays tax at the highest marginal rate, and so the calculation for his CGT commitment is:

$86 000 × 50 per cent × 45 per cent = $19 350.

Terry has a net gain from the property of $66 650.

Evelyn also owns a property worth $200 000, which she too keeps for 10 years. She made the claims for depreciation along the way, receiving a tax benefit of $2350 every year for 10 years.

She sold the property for $300 000, in effect incurring a gain of $100 000. Her buying and selling costs were $14 000, and so her net gain was $86 000. As she had claimed depreciation along the way of $50 000, she was required to make an adjustment for this amount. Evelyn must take the $50 000 from her original purchase price (making it $150 000) and increase her gain by that amount (making it an amount of $136 000 to calculate the gain — real net gain is still $86 000).

As Evelyn held this property for more than 12 months, she qualifies for discounted capital gains tax. She pays tax at the highest marginal rate, and so the calculation for her CGT commitment is:

$136 000 × 50 per cent × 45 per cent = $30 600.

Evelyn has a net gain from the property of $55 400.

At first glance, it would appear that Evelyn has made $11 250 less than Terry. But what about the $23 500 that she claimed along the way as a tax benefit? Add this to the mix and Evelyn's true gain was $78 900, which is $12 250 *more* than Terry made. If you also consider the time value of money (Evelyn received some of this money in the early years when it was worth more) as well as the fact that the cash flow gave her the ability to leverage into more property more quickly, then Evelyn is way ahead of the game, simply because she made the claims for depreciation.

Land tax

In all states of Australia, <u>you will be charged land tax for any landholding outside your principal place of residence</u>, at varying rates, depending on the state. Some states have a tax-free threshold, and in all states you may claim any land tax paid as a tax deduction.

Incurring land tax is not a reason to stop investing. Once you are in a land tax position, there is nothing you can do to alter that except sell, which should not be an option.

You can, however, minimise the amount of land tax you do pay by being aware of the following:

* Land tax is a state by state tax and applies only to land held in that state. <u>Often there is a threshold</u> that incurs no tax. If you <u>spread your investing over all states</u>, it will be a long time before you find yourself in a taxable position in any state and, when you do, it should be minimal.

* Units attract less land tax as they have less land. This is not a reason to buy a unit where there is no demand for units, but where all else is equal, this may be a consideration.

* Land tax is a given. You can plan for it and include it in your calculations. Astute investors should never be

surprised by a land tax bill and you should consider it a cost of investing—a commitment to your future.

Capital gains tax

As previously alluded to, capital gains tax is a fact of investing life in Australia today. Unless it is removed in the future, you can expect to pay capital gains tax on your property gains.

However, it is only payable on realised gains, so while you continue to hold your property, you will not have to pay it. This is as good a reason as any to ensure you adopt a buy and hold strategy for your property investing. You can always leverage against growing equity, so there is rarely a case for selling to realise a gain unless you really want to use it for something else.

There are several different ways to calculate your capital gains tax liability and they are all covered in *How to Maximise Your Property Portfolio* (page 92). The most recent method (currently in use for anyone who has made a purchase after 21 September 1999 and held it for more than 12 months) is:

Sale price less purchase price less allowable costs = gross gain

Gross gain × 50 per cent × your marginal rate of tax
= capital gains tax due

If you do need to sell, try to ensure that you do so in a year where your income is at its lowest. This will reduce the rate of tax applied to the gain. Of course, if you are like me and are convinced that even when you retire you will have a very high taxable income, it is a moot point anyway.

Record keeping

You must keep accurate records of all and any claims you wish to make so that, if asked, you can present evidence as to the authenticity of your claims to the tax office. It is crucial that you know what it is you are doing—relying on your accountant is not good enough, since all taxpayers in Australia are required to be responsible and in charge of their own tax affairs. You cannot hand over this responsibility—even if your accountant makes a mistake, it is you who will be penalised for it.

Getting the tax back, now!

I still meet people who are waiting until the end of the year before they make their tax claims. This is a little like keeping your money under the bed – it does so little for you. When you delay making your claims until the end of the year, you are in essence paying too much tax and allowing the tax office to make use of your money. When it finally gives it back to you, it certainly will not give you any interest on it. It seems silly to let the tax office have money when it asks for it, but not get your tax breaks when you ask for them!

If you have tax benefits to claim, ensure that you complete an Income Tax Withholding Variation (or ITWV form, formerly a 221D form). You can complete these online at www.ato.gov.au (providing you do not have any more than three properties) or print the form and complete it before sending it off.

The form requires you to make estimates about the income, expenses and depreciation you will incur on a property in the coming year. Based on this, the tax you pay through your employer will then be adjusted by the amount of benefits you are entitled to. You will receive your tax benefits every week or fortnight (depending on how you are paid), so that you can use them to reduce your own debt and minimise interest. This money is far better sitting in your loan, offsetting interest, than it is sitting around in consolidated revenue.

Be very careful that you are accurate with your estimates, as you may be penalised for any errors you make. I always like to overestimate the income a little and underestimate the claims, so that if I am wrong it is at least in the tax office's favour.

Summary

- Capital costs are all the costs that relate to buying and selling your property and can only be claimed upon sale.

- Renovations and additions are capital costs.

- Expenses or revenue costs are those costs incurred when generating an income from an investment. They can be claimed each year.

- Division 43 allowances are those claims that relate to the depreciating value of the building.

- Division 42 allowances are those claims which relate to the plant and equipment contained in an income-producing property.

- You should have in place a plan to manage the time when your depreciation allowances have been exhausted.

- You do not have to 'pay back' depreciation, but you do need to make an adjustment for it upon eventual sale. Even so, it is always better to claim it now and adjust later.

- Land tax is a cost of investing—it should not be a reason for you not to invest and you should plan for its eventuality. You can minimise it by spreading your investing among many different states.

- You will incur capital gains tax when you sell any income-producing investment. It can only be avoided by not physically realising your gains—that is, by not selling.

- Keep an accurate record of any claim you make in case the tax office wishes to see it.

- Ensure you get all of the tax benefits available to you as soon as you can by submitting an ITWV form.

Conclusion

Becoming familiar with tax is a must if you are to become a property investor. You simply cannot rely solely on the advice of others, even qualified accountants, as often they miss very important tax claims.

All of the books in my *How to* series cover property investing tax rules in sufficient detail for you to be able to control your own tax affairs.

Chapter 10 _____

And all the rest!

_____

When I write a book, I do it differently to most people and certainly differently to the way my year 12 English teacher would have liked.

I don't start with an outline, from which I write a draft and then, finally, a whole book. Usually, when I think I am ready to write a new book, I sit down with dozens of little pieces of paper and business cards on which I have written titbits of information and numerous insights that may have hit me while speaking to people at expos, and I simply start writing. As I go along, I cross off anything I have written on the scraps, and then write some more. Every few chapters, I print off what I have done and my husband and I read it — I correct spelling and grammar while he adds his thoughts and tells me which bits are good and which are not so good. Then I continue on, crossing off the information as it is added to the book.

It takes me about two weeks, and then I always come to this last chapter and find that there are half a dozen or so things that I really wanted to say, but have not yet found a place for. Hence, the last chapter is always a wonderful collage of things I want you to know that I could not turn into a whole chapter!

Negotiating price

Most people think that they are good negotiators just because they made an offer on a property that was lower than the asking price and, after some to-ing and fro-ing, eventually secured the property for $5000 to $10000 less than what was being asked.

I believe that everyone expects to fetch at least $10000 less than what they have asked for. Therefore, if this is what you pay, you have only really met the expected price.

To be a good negotiator, you have to be unemotional. If you have decided that you really *want* a property, then you will most likely pay far more for it than you should and you will be in the weaker position. If, on the other hand, you make sure that there are several options, and you have no preference for any of them, you can freely and without emotion negotiate on one knowing that if you fail to reach a price, there are plenty of others to choose from. In addition to being unemotional, you must also be hard-nosed, and somewhat uncommunicative.

Let me tell you about two properties my husband and I bought.

One was a block of four strata-titled units. The asking price was $450000 for the four, or $112500 each (same thing, of course). Before even indicating that I might have been interested in making an offer, I tried to get as much information about the vendor as I could. I discovered that she was elderly and in the process of liquidating her substantial property holdings. I also discovered she had a financial adviser giving her his opinion and guiding her in this sale.

My starting offer was $395 000 and it was pretty much laughed at. I ensured that this offer was in writing, as all offers in writing *must* be presented to the vendor, regardless of whether the agent thinks it is likely to be accepted or not. I like vendors to know that a few nibbles are out there, because the sale then becomes more real to them and they may begin to plan for the sale. Once people see a sale in their mind, they become far easier to negotiate with.

The counteroffer was $440 000, and along with it came advice that the vendor would go no lower. I asked the agent to make it known that $400 000 was my final offer (although I actually had in mind a price of somewhere around $415 000). The answer was a flat 'no'. I said 'No deal!' and did not call the agent again.

A week later, he contacted me and said that the vendor would consider $425 000. This was a big drop in price and I gathered that she was now imagining a sale but, having had no other nibbles, figured that I might be her only hope. I countered at $410 000 and advised the agent that any further increases would have to come out of his commission since I was now flat broke! The counteroffer on that was $420 000, so I told the agent I was done, that I had other offers to make and to not ring again unless my $410 000 was accepted.

And it was … two weeks later. Now, I too can be emotional and I must admit that it was a long two weeks. I *so* wanted to call the agent and ask him if he had heard any more, but to do so would show my hand and reveal that I had become involved. I wanted all concerned to think that I cared little about the property and that it was neither here nor there if I succeeded or not.

Similarly, the property we recently bought in Sydney progressed in the same manner. With an asking price of $370 000 and Christmas looming, I was able to discover that the vendors—owner-occupiers—were hoping to upgrade. I knew an offer, any offer, would send them looking for a new home of their own and that, possibly, they too would find a bargain that someone was willing to let go for a little less in view of the low market and bad time of the year.

I was told that there was no way they would accept less than $360 000, and in fact I had confirmed with my son—who works in real estate in the area—that $360 000 was probably close to the money. I told the agent that there was 'no way' that I would be going over $340 000 and I let them go from there. I went away for a week and otherwise made no contact. Over the next four weeks I received two calls from the agent. Each time, he told me that the price was $5000 lower and the vendors were prepared to negotiate. (Ah-ha! Could it be they found something else?!). After two open houses and no other offers, they were getting itchy feet.

My final offer was $345 000 and a 90-day settlement condition (we had to try to raise the money in that time). After a further two weeks, during which I again made no contact with the agent, my offer was accepted, conditions and all. The bank returned a valuation of $350 000 and since these are often lower than market price, I think we pulled off a pretty good deal.

Always go in much lower than anyone else would, have a number of options that you can negotiate on at once and ensure your offers are in writing. Then, wait it out and let them come to you. Progress in very small amounts—by all means increase your offer, but only in $1000 or $2000 lots. And don't think you should be meeting in the middle. All of the negotiations I have made lately have usually seen me come up about 25 per cent of the way and the vendor come down by about 75 per cent. At present, many areas are boasting a buyer's market and there are definitely opportunities available.

Negotiating other costs

As well as negotiating price on property, you can often negotiate the price of the services you require to complete the sale, especially if you are buying property in lots of more than one.

The property we purchased recently was a block of four independently strata-titled units. I began by looking for a building inspector to carry out the pre-purchase inspection. I was quoted anything from $195 per unit to $250 per unit. Eventually, I came across one operator who was willing to negotiate, and he agreed on $450 for the entire four units as long as I arranged for him to inspect them all at once. The pest inspectors were a similar story—most wanted around $200 per unit, until one operator agreed on $125 per unit, again, as long as they could all be done at once.

The big savings came with the stamp duty. If treated as one sale of $410000, the stamp duty would have been $21250. However, had I bought four units in different streets, and settled on them all on the one day, the total stamp duty would have been just $9750. My conveyancer told me he had asked the Office of State Revenue and its representative had insisted that the one larger amount had to be charged. So I took them on myself.

At the Office of State Revenue, Maggie (she refused to reveal her surname) started by telling me there was nothing that could be done. By the end of the conversation, I had her agreeing that, as long as the properties had been offered for separate sale (which they had been, as my agent would later attest to in writing and by producing the original advertisement) and, as long as each one had its own contract (which we then asked for), we could pay the aggregate stamp duty. A little work, investigation and organising on my part and we saved $12000! Of course, Maggie's name and the time and date of our conversation were carefully recorded in the event that I needed them in the future, but it all came off without a hitch.

Always look for the opportunity to negotiate and never accept what you are being told the first time.

Property management

I will admit that property managers can be the bane of your life. I have had my share of problems with property managers and as a group they seem to lack the ability to think outside the square.

However, I am also not prepared nor equipped to conduct the property management myself and I certainly do not think that it pays well enough. On a property attracting $150 a week rent, the management fee is around $13, or around $8 after tax. Work out the hourly rate from that and then decide if you really want to take that on.

You must supervise your manager, especially in the early months, and don't be afraid to sack him or her if he or she does a bad job. Never sign any management contract that has a long termination period; in fact, cross out whatever is there and only agree to a two-week notice of termination period. This should not worry a good manager—you could have a 24-hour termination period and a good manager would not be bothered by it.

A Pocket Guide for Investing in Positive Cash Flow Property (chapter 7) contains an entire chapter on property management, including details on how to recruit the right candidate and then manage him or her. Be very sure you familiarise yourself with this chapter.

Making a positive from a negative

I am often asked if it is possible to turn a negative cash flow property into a positive. The answer is 'probably not'. There is only so much rent you can receive and the costs are usually fairly fixed. There are, however, some things you may be able to do to improve the situation, including the following:

- If you have not had a quantity surveyor prepare a report on the property, do so. For around $500, he or she will identify tax deductions you didn't know existed and this will help with your cash flow.

- Increase the rent by $5. As I mentioned earlier, this will probably not be enough to make someone leave and could help you with your cash flow. Ensure you are charging fair market rent.

- In some cases, a few inexpensive changes could mean more rent. I recently had a property that was being let for $140 a week. I thought this was a little low and, as the tenants were moving, I took the opportunity to advertise to re-lease at $150. Before doing so, I had the place painted ($1000) and re-carpeted ($950). The extra interest on the $1950 to do this was $132 per year, or $2.55 a week. We actually ended up re-letting for $165 a week, $25 more than before. We were $22.50 ahead.

- Some clients have reported being able to increase rent by adding features such as air conditioning and televisions. Always calculate the cost to you in terms of extra interest and work out if the increased rent makes it worthwhile. Don't forget that items like these will add to your depreciation as well.

- Very rarely you may be able to let out your property to students room by room. Often, a house getting $250 a week with four bedrooms can be let out at $80 a room ($320) to students. This is risky though and needs to be closely managed, and you do need to be in an area near a university or college.

Other than these things, a negative cash flow property will remain that way until the rents rise enough to close the gap, possibly years away. You may consider selling and re-buying, or leveraging against any equity into positive cash flow property that makes up the shortfall of the negative one.

I have found a great property — but it is negative

Okay, I am willing to accept that sometimes a great buy comes along and the cash flow is not positive. I cannot condone the buying of property like this, but if you must, ensure that you try the following:

- Clarify the property really does have stunning qualities that will make you money over the long term, and that it is not so negative that a small rate rise or vacancy pushes you to the wall financially.

- Include it in a portfolio where other properties are positive so that they can support this negative one.

- Ascertain how long it will be until the property can become positive through a combination of debt repayment and rent increases. It may be not too far off, in which case your budget may be able to support the property until the time comes.

- Ensure that you do not think it is a great buy purely for emotional reasons. Other people may not agree with your view and you could end up with a 'no cash flow' property — as in one you cannot rent consistently, which then causes severe financial strain.

Don't try to justify the purchase with a host of reasons that really are not valid to property investors. Keep a cool head and be sure you do the research adequately.

My partner does not support me!

We have a wonderful client in Western Australia whose husband was not initially interested in property investing. She went out and did it all herself and, finally, after three purchases, managed to drag him along to one of my seminars. He became instantly motivated and has been a great advocate ever since.

Try not to push an unwilling partner and discuss the option of you going it alone for a while. Be sure that you ask your partner to at least come along to a seminar so that he or she knows what it is you are doing, even if he or she does not want to become involved him- or herself. Try not to be the one who insists that your partner becomes involved—let someone else do that for you by ensuring he or she has exposure, if possible, to expos, shows and the right kind of seminars.

Procrastinating

Every year, I see many of the same investors at the money shows I speak at in all of the states. A lot of them are able to report to me that they have made great progress through the year—adding to their portfolios with great cash flow properties and working solidly toward their financial futures.

Others tell me how they have read all of my books, been to dozens of seminars and still they cannot find the courage to get started. Others still tell me that they genuinely want to buy real estate, but they just can't find that 'perfect' property.

You will never buy your second property until you have bought your first. Additionally, that 'perfect' property is just not going to be there. The first property we ever bought was far from perfect, but it got us started. While the 20 must ask questions are crucial to every transaction, don't get so caught up in your purchase being perfect that you miss out on what may be a pretty viable investment after all.

For those who worry about making any move at all, you must do what I did—imagine the worst possible thing that could happen in your life, and then accept that a poor property investment will never be as bad as that! It won't kill you and, if it is that bad, you can always sell it and start again. I end all of my seminars with the quote: 'Another day you wait is another day you waste', and I guarantee that once you do start, you will wish you had done so years sooner.

Find a mentor

We all need mentors in our lives who can lift us when we are down and provide us with an example to follow. They can also support us and guide us when we need it most. Having information and opportunity is one thing, but few people have the internal motivation to keep doing the best they can do, and so need guidance during those tough times.

Be careful of some companies that offer help with property investment, as few can really offer the kind of support you need. If you do decide to use a professional advising company, be sure that property investing is its genuine field of expertise and that you ask its staff for testimonials from real clients whose existence you can confirm. Lastly, do not take advice from someone who has a financial interest in the property he or she is recommending to you—this cannot possibly be considered independent advice.

Does the property have to be new to get tax benefits?

As long as the property was built after 1987, you can claim the balance of the building depreciation. Also, in any property you purchase, you can make a claim for any renovations or additions carried out after 1992. Plant and equipment on any

how does this work?

property are given a 'new effective life' by the quantity surveyor when he or she prepares his or her report, and so you can begin to claim depreciation all over again.

Invest or owner-occupy?

Frequently, people who have yet to own any real estate ask me if it is better for them to buy a home in which to live, or a property in which to invest. The answer to this question depends on personal preferences. Some people like to have a place to call their own, to decorate as they see fit and live in without the worry of having a landlord. These people may be best to buy a property to live in, ensuring that as soon as they can they use any equity they have acquired as leverage for an investment property. Others don't care too much one way or another and so these people are considering the greater financial benefits available to them by investing in property elsewhere while they live in rental accommodation in the area of their choice. Where you have the means to do either (invest first or owner-occupy first), you must do the calculations to assess the best way to proceed. If you bear in mind that any property growth can be used as leverage for more property, you may well find that there is little financial difference in either option.

Aside from considering your personal preference and working out which is the best option, it may also come down to where you actually want to settle down. I have met couples who have a dream to live in a particular, expensive suburb, yet they are still many years away from having enough of a deposit to buy a home in that area. For these people, rather than simply waiting while they save (and watch properties everywhere continue to increase in value), I always suggest that they use the savings they have already to purchase an investment property which is at the cheaper end of the market (positive cash flow, of course). Then, while they continue to save, they have the benefits of both the increasing savings and the growing equity in the investment property. Depending on how much they need to put together for their owner-occupied residence, they can continue to buy cheaper investment properties while they save for their own home. Then the time will come when their savings *plus* the equity they have accumulated in property is enough to buy their own home. Let's look at the following example:

Michelle and Jake had savings of $25000. They wanted to live in a suburb where the average house price is around $400000. To access a loan at 80 per cent of the value (and so avoid lender's mortgage insurance, which would be costly at this level of borrowing), they need to save $80000 plus costs of around $15000, a total of $95000. Despite being excellent savers, they are only managing to set aside $20000 a year and so are still around four years away from achieving their goal. By the time they save the required amount, the property they want may have increased in value. Even if it has only increased by 4 per cent per annum, it will still cost over $60000 more, meaning that Michelle and Jake will need a further $15000. In reality, they are five years from acquiring their home.

Rachel and Ben had the same amount of savings and a similar capacity to save. They used their $25000 to purchase a positive cash flow property valued at $100000 (with a loan of $80000). This property had a $20-a-week positive cash flow.

After 15 months, they purchased a second property of the same value and cash flows, and, after 30 months, they purchase a third. They now have three properties and continue to save.

After three-and-a-half years (42 months), their position is as follows:

- They have savings of $12 500 (saved for the six months since the past purchase).

- Property 1 is worth $118 643 (assuming a 5 per cent growth). Their equity is $38 643.

- Property 2 is worth $110 250. Their equity is $30 250.

- Property 3 is worth $105 000. Their equity is $25 000.

- Positive cash flow of $20 per week. Each property has provided extra savings of $7040.

Rachel and Ben's total equity is $93 893 which at 80 per cent allows them to borrow $75 000. Added to their savings of $12 500 and their cash flow of $7040, they have a total of $95 450. The property purchases have allowed them to save more quickly, as they have had the exposure to growth assets to assist them.

[handwritten marginalia: this would mean that this loan would be non-tax deductible as they would be buying a personal property!?]

The most important thing to remember when making the choice of whether to invest or owner-occupy first, is that, as soon as you obtain a property of some description, you leverage against its equity (as soon as there is some) to buy more property.

Diamonds in the rough

Always remember that, since on-paper deductions vary from property to property, each individual property will have a different amount of tax deductions than another.

When we purchased in Airlie Beach, it seemed that most properties had increased in value to the point where it would be hard to find one with a positive cash flow. However, we eventually discovered one property that had been internally stripped and totally renovated. The raw cash flow was negative, but the huge amount of deductions turned it into a positive cash flow.

While it is true that some areas will have more positive cash flow than others (due to proportionately higher rent returns), don't fall into the trap of only searching in known positive cash flow areas. You could find a positive cash flow property just about anywhere! When you do find it, don't buy all of your properties there. A good spread across locations is always paramount.

Conclusion

Well, that's it from me for now. Enjoy your investing and don't be afraid to email me with any questions you have. Do be sure to become a Destiny® VIP and receive the newsletters and seminar discounts as well as free expo tickets whenever we can secure them. Associate with positive people and soak up as much good quality education as you can. All of the branch managers at Destiny® are there to help you and some of our services are free of charge, so it is always worth checking out what your local branch can do for you before trying to navigate the shark-infested waters on your own.

And, most importantly of all, never give up. So many people will tell you that you are making a mistake or try to tempt you with strategies that simply will not work. Be true to yourself, be ethical, work hard and you will be the one who succeeds where others fail.

And be sure to have fun along the way. I certainly do!

Which book is for you?

_____

I have written a number of books about investing in positive cash flow property and I have made a point of ensuring each one mainly contains new information. I did not intend to do it that way — each time I write a new book, I am convinced I have shared everything I know — and I usually have. The books tend to reflect my personal journey through property investing and each time I learn new things, I just want to share them with everyone!

Each book is designed to suit investors at different stages of their investing life. To help you decide which one(s) you should read, I have provided an outline of each and who they are meant for.

How to Make Your Money Last as Long as You Do

As the first book I ever wrote about positive cash flow property, *How to Make Your Money Last as Long as You Do* explains in basic terms what the concept is all about. In addition, it covers personal financial management, managing debt, rapid mortgage reduction, basic tax information and information about buying and selling real estate. It also looks in-depth at banks and borrowing.

You should read this book if you have a personal home loan debt that you would like to manage better and if you are new to the world of property investing.

How to Make Your Money Last as Long as You Do is also available in a New Zealand edition that outlines New Zealand tax benefits.

How to Create an Income for Life

This book is the A to Z guide to investing in positive cash flow property and is without a doubt my most popular book. It covers in great depth the concepts of positive cash flow property, taxation information for investors, property management, loan structuring, and property types and their risk ratings. It explores serviced apartments and other such unusual property types and looks at wealth protection.

You should read this book if you already have your personal debt under control and want to start, continue or change the way you put together a property portfolio.

How to Maximise Your Property Portfolio

Some people want to know more than their accountants and if this is you, this book is a must. It does not, however, replace the two previous books and depends upon you having already read at least one of them.

How to Maximise Your Property Portfolio covers the debate about cash flow and capital growth and puts the two into context. It provides advanced information about assessing cash flows and details body corporate information.

It also takes a look at niche market property and its place in a portfolio. The book then goes on to examine portfolio management and outlines exit strategies.

The tax information contained in *How to Maximise Your Property Portfolio* is more advanced and covers the methods of depreciation and low value pooling. It looks at structures such as companies and trusts, and explores which names property should be held in and why. Lastly, it looks at property management with a detailed section on recruiting a property manager.

You should read this book after you read one of the other two and when you have started to put together your property portfolio.

A Pocket Guide to Investing in Positive Cash Flow Property

Actually, you would need an extremely large pocket to fit this book in — once I started writing it, I just couldn't stop!

The reference to 'pocket guide' is more about how to use it than it is about its size. After having written the other three books, many readers told of how they were full of great information that they then needed to disseminate into a process they could follow.

So, I decided to do this for them. A *Pocket Guide* is not an educational book, as such. Rather, it is a process guide. It relies on the fact that you have already gained the knowledge from reading the other books and it gives you a step by step guide for the actual buying process. Each chapter is a new step and once you have read the entire book you *will* own a property.

I use it myself every time I make a new purchase, just to make sure that I do not miss any steps. A *Pocket Guide to Investing in Positive Cash Flow Property* contains formulas, calculators, pro forma documents to photocopy for your bank and lawyer, and a checklist at the end of each step to make sure you have completed the step fully.

Again, it will not teach you new information — it will simply organise the information you do have into a logical step by step plan. You will need to read one of the first two books before getting to A *Pocket Guide*.

Your risk profile

_____

The following questions will help you identify your risk profile as it applies to property investing. Select one answer in each section.

How would you describe yourself?

1. Retired and dependent on existing funds and/or pensions for income.

2. With a family to support. While you understand the need to invest, you cannot see how it will be possible, as your income is fully committed to the family budget.

3. Easily managing your current financial commitments. Your current income provides an acceptable lifestyle. You may be just starting out on your career or be well-established.

4. At the peak of your career and income, possibly with a dual income. You either have no dependants or can easily manage the expense needs of your dependants.

What is your understanding of investing in property?

1. You are not very familiar with it.

2. You understand the need to invest, but not much else.

3. You understand how different property types can produce differing income and growth.

4. You are an experienced investor with a current property portfolio.

What are your financial goals?

1. Income from an investment is the most important thing to you.

2. Safety is the most important feature for you.

3. You have a specific time frame of, say, five years and a set return you would like to achieve in that time.

4. Growth is the most important thing to you.

If your property was to suddenly lose value by 20 per cent, what would your reaction be?

1. You would sell up immediately and never invest in property again.

2. You would keep what you had, but not buy any more.

3. You would be concerned, but would wait for a while before you invested again.

4. You would not be concerned — you might even invest in the same area again while you can still get a bargain!

Which of the following options do you prefer?

1. Stable, though low, returns.

2. Consistent returns with minimal tax savings.

3. Variable returns with good tax savings.

4. Higher returns with maximum tax savings (but higher risk).

When do you plan to retire?

1. Already retired.

2. Within five years.

3. In five to 15 years.

4. In more than 15 years.

How often do you sell your property?

1. Never.

2. Within 10 years.

3. Every time there is a substantial gain.

4. Every year or two.

In relation to buying property unseen, you feel:

1. You simply could not do it.

2. You may be able to do it if you saw lots of pictures of the property.

3. You would be happy to do it if you arranged for someone trustworthy to go and look at it.

4. You don't need to see it at all, as long as the figures stack up.

Use the following formula to add up your score, then check your results overleaf.

For every 1 answer, score one point.

For every 2 answer, score two points.

For every 3 answer, score three points.

For every 4 answer, score four points.

Your results

0-8 points: Conservative

Preserving your capital is your most important consideration. You have a short-term investment period in which income and capital stability is of prime concern. You should invest in low-risk property, which includes standard residential property in well-populated city suburbs or large regional towns. You should ensure a low 'loan to valuation ratio' (LVR), say, around 50 to 60 per cent.

8–12 points: Stable

Your investment term is three to five years and you are willing to take a small degree of short-term risk if it means the chance of long-term returns. Security is very important to you, though, and income is more important than growth. You should buy standard residential property and you may be able to buy in smaller towns with economic vibrancy, such as mining towns. You can comfortably set your LVR at 80 per cent.

13–21 points: Balanced

You have a relatively long period in which to invest and are comfortable with short-term volatility for long-term growth and income. That is, you would like some security but are prepared to take some risk. You could invest in standard residential, short-term holiday lets with standard management and some commercial premises, such as offices with high demand. LVR should be set at 80 per cent.

22–28 points: Assertive

You look for growth investments and are willing to include some speculative investments. You can cope with negative returns and increased volatility. Capital growth is your prime concern. You can invest in inner city apartments (may have high growth) or niche market properties such as serviced apartments and retirement villages (high income), as well as factories and warehouses. You could stand up to a 90 per cent LVR if necessary. High income earners may stand negative cash flow.

Glossary

ASIC: Australian Securities & Investments Commission.

Body corporate: An owners' committee with owners volunteering for positions. In place to manage funds collected to maintain common property in strata titled properties.

Borrower: A party to a loan — the person borrowing the funds.

Capital costs: Costs incurred when purchasing a property as well as those paid for structural improvements.

Capital gain: The profit made on an investment.

Capitalising: Allowing the interest on a loan to build up without paying any repayments at all. The loan balance will increase.

Commission (real estate): Fee payable to a real estate agent (or other salesperson) for selling a property by the person authorising the sale. Usually a percentage of the sale price, or can be a set fee where a relationship between the developer and salesperson exists.

Contract of sale: Written agreement setting out the terms and conditions of a property sale.

Conveyancing: Legal process of transferring the ownership of a property from one person to another. Can be carried out by either a property solicitor, a conveyancer or a settlement agent.

Deposit: Usually 5 to 10 per cent of the purchase price of a property placed in trust upon exchange or signing of the contract.

Depreciation: Where the original cost of an item is progressively written off over its effective life.

Equity: The difference between what you owe and what you own of a property.

Fittings and fixtures: Items such as baths, stoves, lights and other fittings, kitchen, linen or storage cupboards or wardrobes. Fittings are not normally included in a contract if they can be removed without causing damage.

Forecast: Assumptions made (often on paper by developers) about the future growth and income earning potential of an investment, based on historical performance and projected future events.

Gross income: Income earned before tax and any costs.

Guarantor: A party to a loan who is not a borrower. A guarantor provides a guarantee for the debt to be paid in the event that the borrower defaults. Often a guarantor provides security for a debt for someone else.

Interest: The sum charged by the lender, calculated on the outstanding balance of borrowings, in deference to having supplied you with funds.

Interest-only loans: A loan on which interest only is paid periodically and the principal is paid at the end of the term.

Investment: The purchase of a security with the ultimate goal of producing capital gain or an income.

Joint tenants: Joint tenancy is the equal holding of property by two or more persons. When one party dies, the remaining tenants share the portion owned by the deceased.

Land tax: Value-based levy applied to some property. Varies from state to state.

Landlord: The owner of an investment property.

Lease: A document granting possession of a property for a given period without conferring ownership. The lease document specifies the terms and conditions of occupancy by the tenant.

Leverage: To utilise the growth in any one investment vehicle to invest into more vehicles.

Mortgage: Legal agreement on the terms and conditions of a loan for the purpose of buying real estate, whereby the person offering the mortgage takes security over property.

Negative gearing: The writing off of investment property losses where a negative cash flow results — that is, expenses exceed income.

Net income: In-hand income after tax and costs.

Net profit: Remaining funds left after all costs are paid.

Niche market property: Property that is zoned residential but provided for specific markets — such as tourism, retirement or student.

Occupancy: Period that a tenant occupies a property.

On-paper deductions: Tax claimable items that do not have a relative cash outlay.

Owner-occupied: Property in which the owners reside — that is, non-income-producing property.

Positive cash flow: The net positive income earned on a property after adding rent plus tax breaks and deducting actual property costs.

Positive gearing: Where income on an investment property exceeds expenses and tax must be paid on the gain.

Principal: The original amount of money that has been borrowed not considering accruing interest.

Repayment: The amount required by a lender to repay a loan, including its interest, within a set period of time.

Revenue costs: Costs incurred to earn income on an investment property.

Risk profile: Outlines the level of risk an investor can stand according to questions they answer about how they feel about investing and their personal investing choices.

Security: Property offered to the mortgagee in return for a loan.

Settlement: Completion of sale (or advancing of a loan) when the balance of a contract price is paid to the vendor and the buyer is legally entitled to take possession of the property.

Stamp duty: A state government tax imposed on the sale of real estate.

Strata title: Most commonly used for flats and units, this title gives you ownership of a small piece of a larger property and includes common property.

Tax: An amount of money paid to the government as a percentage of each dollar earned.

Tax benefits: Any allowable item that reduces the amount of tax you must pay.

Taxable income: Income on which tax is paid after allowable deductions have been considered.

Tenancy in common: The holding of property by two or more persons, with either equal shares or unequal shares. If one person dies, the property is dealt with in accordance with the will.

Tenant: Either the person signing a lease to occupy premises or the description of a party to a property title.

Term: The time length of a loan.

Title: Legal proof of ownership of a property, carrying the owner's name and other information.

Vacancy: Period of time a property is without a tenant.

Valuation: Assessment of the value of a property given in a written report by a registered valuer.

Valuer: A person licensed to give an estimation of the value of property.

Vendor: Person offering a property for sale.

Index

Destiny®Financial Solutions

1. Investment seminars

Margaret Lomas frequently conducts evening seminars around the country. The aim of the seminars is to provide clarity on information contained in Margaret's books and to allow attendees the chance to have their personal questions answered. To find out about the next seminar in your state, visit **www.destiny.net.au** or phone **1800 648 640**.

Watch the website for more information about all Destiny® events.

2. Personal support and assistance

Destiny® Financial Solutions is expanding its network to provide personal assistance by trained branch staff in many areas throughout Australia. We can assist you to put together a personalised property investing strategy that is not reliant on the purchase of a particular property. All of our branches offer financial advising support and assistance for direct property investors. Phone or email us, or visit the website to find out our branch locations or to ask about the unique services we can offer.

To discover more, visit **www.destiny.net.au**

3. Free download — Destiny® FinSoft

All readers qualify for this unique program which calculates cash flow for you and provides an abundance of other calculators and useful website links.

Phone **1800 648 640** or for email instructions contact: **download@destiny.net.au**

4. Join the Destiny® team

Do you possess a passion for property investment and have a genuine interest in helping others to achieve their financial goals?

Destiny® Financial Solutions is an innovative national company that has carved out a unique position in the financial services landscape.

A pioneer of the property investment industry, Destiny® assists clients to achieve prosperity using direct residential property as the vehicle.

With massive plans for further growth, we are looking for the right people to play their part in our future success.

At Destiny®, we are committed to:

- absolute integrity in all client dealings
- a culture of ethics and honesty
- a people-first attitude
- making a positive contribution to the community.

Would you make an outstanding participant in a business opportunity based on these philosophies?

For more information on business opportunities offered by Destiny® visit our website at **www.destiny.net.au**. Alternatively, you can email Destiny® Managing Director Reuben Lomas on **reuben.lomas@destiny.net.au**

Thank you for reading this book. We can be contacted at:
info@destiny.net.au

For assistance with your finance needs, contact:
finance@destiny.net.au

For download instructions, contact:
download@destiny.net.au

If you would like to tell us how you felt about this book or make a suggestion for future books, please contact:
margaret.lomas@destiny.net.au

Destiny®Financial Solutions

PO Box 5400
Chittaway Bay NSW 2261
Ph: 1800 648 640
www.destiny.net.au

'Destiny' and 'DestinyTrack' are registered trademarks of Destiny Business Solutions P/L and are used by permission. All rights reserved.